NUMBER THREE

*Essays on the American West*, no. 3

*sponsored by the*
*Elma Dill Russell Spencer Foundation*

*America's Frontier Culture*

**THREE ESSAYS**

# America's Frontier Culture

## THREE ESSAYS

### Ray A. Billington

*Foreword by*
*W. Turrentine Jackson*

**TEXAS A&M UNIVERSITY PRESS**
*College Station and London*

Library of Congress Cataloging in Publication Data

Billington, Ray Allen, 1903–
   America's frontier culture.

   (Essays on the American West; no. 3)
   CONTENTS: The American frontiersman.—The frontier and American culture.—Cowboys, Indians, and the
land of promise.—Bibliography (p.       )
      1. Frontier and pioneer life—The West—Addresses,
essays, lectures. 2. Indians of North America—The West—
Addresses, essays, lectures. 3. Cowboys—The West—Addresses, essays, lectures. 4. The West—History—Addresses,
essays, lectures. I. Title. II. m Series.
F596.B46       978       77-89510
   ISBN 0-89096-036-4

*Manufactured in the United States of America*

FIRST EDITION

To
Mary Isabel Fry

who has helped make the Huntington
Library an academic paradise for a
generation of scholars—including
the author of this book

# Contents

# *Foreword*

GENERATIONS ago Frederick Jackson Turner sought
an explanation of American institutions and character
in the frontier experience. As waves of subduers of the
wilderness, followed by pioneer settlers, moved westward across the American continent, characteristic national institutions emphasizing opportunity and op-
portunism, individualism and democracy, and upward
social mobility were forged. Distinguishing characteristics of the American people that emerged from the
three-century-long process of westering, according to
Turner, included optimism, resourcefulness, enthusiasm, and at the same time crudeness, impatience, and
materialism. In the years of discussion and debate concerning Turner's hypothesis about the significance of
the frontier in American life, no individual has written
more, or more effectively, to explicate the life and ideas
of Turner than Ray Allen Billington.

Turner and his supporters have been characterized
as environmental determinists. In the struggle of man
against nature, the wilderness overcame the pioneer.
Initially the frontiersman found it necessary to abandon
the civilized life and institutions he had known; only

later was he able to rebuild society with distinguishable modifications. In his Harmsworth inaugural lecture, "The American Frontiersman," Billington has selected the most obvious example—the mountain man of the fur trade era—as an example of Turner's suggested reversion to the primitive. Traveling far beyond the frontier of settlement, these men, searching the wilds of the West for furs, were in some cases outcasts from civilized society, picturesque wanderers in the wilderness, whose life, according to Billington, was concerned with three things: beaver, buffalo, and Indians. While leading a semisavage life, they salvaged enough of previous experience in a more civilized society to maintain their superiority. However, the impact of the environment led to uniqueness in the food they ate, the clothes they wore, their speech, and their mental attitudes. Perhaps to a lesser degree other frontiersmen—cattlemen, miners, and farmers—also renounced aspects of the old civilization only to build a new one as the years passed. Thus, as Billington suggested to his listeners in Oxford, there emerged a society in the United States quite different from that in England.

Students of the frontier process have been profoundly disturbed by the inconsistencies and enigmas found in Turner's writing. How could the West, evolving as a section with unique characteristics and interests, stimulate the growth of nationalism? How could frontiersmen emphasize the importance of individualism and cooperation at the same time? How could they be innovators and still emphasize conformity, and talk of idealism and simultaneously practice materialism? How could they boast of egalitarianism and upward social mobility without recognizing the contradiction? Perhaps the most difficult of Turner's ideas to reconcile was the suggestion that pioneers improved civilization in the process of abandoning it. In his address to the California Library Association, "The Frontier and American Culture," Billington has undertaken the task of reconciling this conflict of ideas while admitting that the task is not a simple one. He suggests that many backwoodsmen did, in fact, "secede from civilization" and live a hedonistic life, but the indolent and reprobate were in the minority among frontiersmen. Those who took up the land, both rancher and farmer, were the vast majority, and a significant number of these people made a heroic effort to perpetuate the life and culture they had known in the East. Churches, schools, subscription libraries, and the theater were supported far more extensively than the wealth of the communities justified. Even some trappers, cowboys, and miners had a desire for learning that matched that of the families of the cattlemen and farmers. In analyzing the reading habits of the pioneers, Billington suggests that they selected traditional literary works, rather than more practical treatises, probably as escapism from the harsh reality of their lives. But by and large frontiersmen were men of action, not contemplation. Many had no concern for learning or for books, and undoubtedly anti-intellectualism was one of the traits that these frontiersmen bestowed upon the nation.

Another group of scholars concerned with the westward movement has dealt with the myth and the reality of that experience. No matter what the facts, the romantic image of the American frontier has penetrated the national conscience and is firmly implanted there. In his address to the International Congress of the Historical Sciences, Billington presented the evidence to prove that this myth is not limited to the United States but is a worldwide phenomenon. Two facets of the myth appear to dominate: the equation of masculinity with lawlessness, violence, repulsiveness, and savagery on the one hand, and on the other the myth of the Garden of Eden, the land with abundant resources of nature ripe for exploitation, the gateway to material wealth, political freedom, and upward social mobility. Among the perpetrators of these myths were western travelers, novelists, guidebook authors, and land agents of various sorts. In their writings they noted the unorthodox clothing, the abominable manners, the brutality, and the constant boasting of frontier residents while simultaneously praising a land of prosperity, liberty, equality, even egalitarianism where, for better or for worse, subservience had been eliminated. Historians know that people act on the basis of what they believe to be true, no matter how mistaken, as often as on the foundations of truth. Billington suggests that this dual image of the American frontier was a factor, among many greater ones, that encouraged a spirit of change and even revolt in the western world during the late nineteenth and early twentieth centuries. Liberals everywhere emphasized the evolution of democratic institutions identified with the frontier experience and the higher standard of living in the United States and therefore urged change; conservatives emphasized the unique circumstance of the presence in the American West of abundant, cheap land, which they claimed was responsible for equality and prosperity, and insisted that it could not be duplicated elsewhere.

Some western historians feel compelled to enter a demurrer to Billington's preoccupation with Turner's concepts of the frontier experience, and a new generation of historians, quite logically, is looking at the American West from a different vantage point than that of Turner or Billington, yet no one is more aware of the fact that there is a new day in scholarship among western historians than Ray Allen Billington, and no one has been more supportive of younger historians. The masterful studies that follow offer ample proof that Billington is without peer in the comprehension and elaboration of the frontier experience as Frederick Jackson Turner first wrote about it. He has often been hailed as the "dean" of western historians. All the enviable hallmarks of Billington's historical writing are there: crystal clear organization, dramatic and exciting style, the phrase worth repeating, the bold and sweeping interpretation, and most important, the text that is a joy to read.

W. Turrentine Jackson

*University of California, Davis*
*May, 1977*

*America's Frontier Culture*
THREE ESSAYS

# The American Frontiersman

Those who seek to explain the distinctive characteristics of the American people and their institutions can find the answer not in any single factor, but in the multiplicity of forces that have helped to create the unique civilization of the United States. The European heritage, the continuing impact of ideas from abroad, the mingling of peoples, the spread of the industrial revolution, and the growth of class consciousness have all played their role in producing "the American, this new man." Yet of these molding forces, none was more important than the environment, which reshaped the transplanted civilizations of the Old World into the distinctive cultural pattern of the United States.

The most unique feature of that environment was the presence in America of an area of unlimited opportunity lying always to the west of the settled portions of

Delivered as "The American Frontiersman: A Case Study in Reversion to the Primitive," inaugural lecture as Harold Vyvyan Harmsworth Professor of History before the University of Oxford, February 2, 1954, and subsequently published by the Clarendon Press, Oxford, 1954.

the continent. There—where a king's ransom in furs could be had for the taking, where lush grasslands beckoned the herdsman, where fortunes in gold and silver lay scarcely hidden, where fertile lands waited only the magic touch of man to produce their wealth—men and women could begin life anew with only their brains and brawn and courage to sustain them. There waited the riches that fate had denied them in older societies; there they could realize the social equality that has been man's goal since the dawn of the modern era. Through the history of America this western land—this frontier—has lured men and women westward in wave after wave of eager homeseekers.

As they moved, alone or in small groups, they carried with them the habits, the institutions, and the cultural baggage of the stratified societies they had left behind. In the western wilderness these relics of civilization were out of place; highly developed political institutions were unnecessary in a tiny frontier outpost; complex economic systems were useless in an isolated community geared to an economy of self-sufficiency; rigid social customs were outmoded in a land where prestige depended on skill with the ax or rifle rather than on hereditary glories. So there occurred in each of these frontier communities a rapid reversion to the primitive. Simple associations of the settlers provided such governmental controls as existed; each man cared for his own economic needs without dependence on his fellows; cultural progress halted as the frontiersmen concentrated on the primal tasks of providing food, clothing, and shelter for their families. In this reversion toward a state of nature, the habits and customs of older civilizations were momentarily forgotten.

Gradually newcomers drifted in to swell the population of each wilderness outpost. As their numbers increased, the community began a slow climb back toward civilization once more. Governmental controls were tightened and extended, economic specialization set in, social stratification began, and cultural activities quickened. The process continued until eventually a fully developed society evolved. This new society, however, differed from the old from which it had sprung. The accident of separate evolution, the borrowings from the different lands represented among its founders, and the influence of the physical environment in which it had developed all played their part in creating a unique social organism, similar to but differing from the older civilizations that lay to the east.

As this process went on, over and over again, during the three centuries required to settle the continent, these minute organisms slowly merged into a national society as unique as the units from which it was formed. The characteristics of its people and the nature of its institutions reflected their primitive origins long after the frontier had passed on westward. An "Americanization" of both men and society had taken place. The distinctive traits that are associated with the American people of today—their dislike of governmental interference in their economic affairs, their materialism, their mobility, their inventiveness, their willing acceptance of innovation, their faith in political and social democracy, their rabid nationalism, their unabashed faith in continued progress—these are characteristics that stemmed at least partly from the frontier environment in which the United States grew to maturity.

To demonstrate the truth of these generalizations—to demonstrate, in other words, the contribution of the frontier to the uniqueness of American civilization—the historian must be able to show that the transition to a wilderness way of life forced the frontiersmen to abandon their inherited cultures so completely that the civilization to which they eventually returned borrowed little from their past experiences. All the frontier types that aided in the conquest of the American West—the gold miners, the cattlemen, and the pioneer farmers—exhibited the corrosive influence of a forest environment on imported cultures, but none showed that influence better than the fur trappers who skimmed the first wealth from the land as they marched westward across the continent. At the point where those trappers made their last stand against the advancing agricultural frontier—in the Rocky Mountain country during the two decades after 1825—this reversion to the primitive occurred to a degree unknown elsewhere. The half-civilized, half-savage pioneers who roamed the West in search of beaver during those years were the supreme examples of the destructive impact of the wilderness on inherited traits and institutions.

The vast distances of the Far West were responsible. When the exploitation of the region's furs began, the frontier of farms and villages had only just crossed the Mississippi River. Beyond lay a thousand miles of treeless prairies, and beyond those rose the forested slopes of the Rocky Mountain range, where beaver abounded in swift-flowing streams. To send brigades of trappers westward to the fur country each year proved impracticable, for the expenses of the long journey absorbed all profits. The only answer was to establish trappers permanently in the mountains and bring them needed supplies yearly. The inauguration of this system, in the middle 1820's, launched the era of the mountain men in the history of the American West. For the next two decades five or six hundred of these trappers lived constantly in the mountains, roaming far and wide in pursuit of beaver and renewing contact with the world they had forsaken only when the caravan of laden pack mules arrived each summer from Saint Louis. Living far in advance of the frontier of settlement, they were the men who were destined to demonstrate that the American pioneer could discard the cloak of civilization almost completely.

The pattern of their lives varied little from year to year, but was never monotonous. Singly or in little bands of three or four, and always with their Indian wives, they began their yearly tasks each spring by searching promising streams for telltale signs that would indicate the presence of beaver. Each felled cottonwood was scanned for marks of the animals' sharp teeth; each mud flat was surveyed for the characteristic tracks of the beaver paw. When "sign" was found, the hunters set their traps with a skill that Indians envied; wading into the river at a distant point, they splashed water over their footmarks to hide tracks and scent, placed the trap with an unerring instinct at the exact spot where the musky-smelling castorum bait would attract their prey, secured the trap's long chain to a heavy log so it could not be dragged into deep water, affixed a floating stick to mark its location, and left the stream with all the precautions they had used in entering.[1] This process was repeated until each had set as many as a dozen traps. The following morning they were back again, keeping a sharp eye out for Indian "sign," to remove the shining peltry and reset the traps. Gradually they worked their way up the streams, trapping constantly as they followed the advance of spring from low-lying valleys to mountain heights. Not until late June, when the warm summer sun started the animals shedding and ruined their pelts, did the "spring hunt" come to an end.

Then the trappers from all the mountains turned their steps toward the annual rendezvous. The site had been selected a year before and the word passed around among the mountain men. Always some sheltered spot was chosen where towering mountain ranges protected the trappers from wind and cold and where grass and water were plentiful. They might gather beneath the sandstone cliffs of the Wind River range, where the valleys of the Popo Agie and Wind rivers were green with waving grass and bright with flaming wildflowers; perhaps Pierre's Hole was the favoured spot, where the stark nakedness of the snow-dappled Grand Tetons awed even the wilderness-jaded frontiersmen; perhaps they had agreed to meet on the sun-baked plain that bordered the still waters of the Great Salt Lake. To this designated spot came flocking the bearded mountain

[1]Contemporary descriptions of trapping methods are in Frances F. Victor, *River of the West* (Hartford, 1870), pp. 64–65; George F. Ruxton, *Life in the Far West* (Norman, Okla., 1951), pp. 75–76; and Albert Pike, *Prose Sketches and Poems* (Boston, 1834), pp. 33–34.

men from all the West with their pack mules laden with beaver peltry, dark-skinned Mexicans from Taos and Santa Fe, French-Canadian deserters from England's Hudson's Bay Company, and whole villages of friendly Indians, who pitched their tepees and settled down to join in the fun. Often more than six hundred trappers and as many Indians met together at the annual rendezvous.

Shortly after the first of July the caravan of trading goods arrived from Saint Louis. The mountain men always rode out to meet the mile-long line of laden mules, yelling like demons as they greeted the merchants who were willing to endure the wearisome journey for profits of 2,000 percent on their investments.[2] They asked eagerly for year-old news first, then watched greedily as the merchandise was spread before them: powder from the Du Pont works in Delaware, lead from the mines of the Galena district of Illinois, sturdy rifles from the shops of Missouri gunsmiths, knives from the Green River Works in Massachusetts, beaver traps from England's bustling factories, beads and trinkets from Italy, coffee and sugar from South America, blankets from New England's textile mills, hanks of tobacco from Kentucky, and cask after cask of raw alcohol from the distilleries of Cincinnati.

Trading came first as trappers exchanged their "hairy bank notes," the beaver skins, for needed supplies or rare luxuries or finery for their squaws. Then the flat

[2]Osburne Russell, *Journal of a Trapper; or, Nine Years in the Rocky Mountains, 1834–1843* (Boise, Idaho, 1921), pp. 62–63; Joseph Williams, *Narrative of a Tour from the State of Indiana to the Oregon Territory in the Years 1841–2* (Cincinnati, 1843), p. 14.

casks of alcohol were tapped, and the rendezvous was turned into a scene of roaring debauchery. Day after day, night after night, the trappers passed metal camp kettles of the lethal fluid about until not a sober person could be found. Some gambled recklessly when drunk, for there were no misers among men who faced death daily; often they squandered away in a few hours their entire year's earnings, their rifles, their horses, their Indian wives, and in a few cases their own scalps.[3] Others raced their horses or staged wrestling matches with no holds barred. Fights were common and, as drunkenness increased, often fatal. Occasionally duels were fought, usually with rifles at twenty paces, with one or both participants sure to be killed.[4] Sometimes the fights became general and resulted in a large loss of life.[5] But eventually both the alcohol and the mountain men were exhausted. Those who had gambled away their guns and horses pledged their next year's catch for new supplies, and all stumbled away into the wilderness, their year's earnings squandered in a few days of barbaric dissipation.

For a few weeks afterward the mountain men enjoyed a vacation as they recovered from the effects of the rendezvous, but with the cooler days of September at hand the "fall hunt" began. Starting high on mountain streams where the frosty nights first restored the quality of the beaver fur, they worked their way down the rivers

[3]George F. Ruxton, *Adventures in Mexico and the Rocky Mountains* (London, 1849), pp. 245–246.

[4]Such a duel is described in Samuel Parker, *Journal of an Exploring Tour Beyond the Rocky Mountains* (Ithaca, 1838), pp. 79–80.

[5]James B. Marsh, *Four Years in the Rockies; or, the Adventures of Isaac P. Rose* (New Castle, Pa., 1884), pp. 97–107.

until the last stream was frozen and the last beaver hibernating. Then the trappers scattered to their winter camps. Some settled in groups in Brown's Hole of the Green River or the sheltered valley of the Big Horn or some other protected spot beyond the mountains.[6] Others joined their wives' Indian tribes to spend the winter months among the Indians. Still more established lonely camps on the banks of mountain streams, where they lived cozily with their squaws in skin lodges, venturing out only to bring in the game needed for food.[7] With the first sign of spring they stirred into action; traps were cleaned, rifles checked, moccasins and buckskin hunting shirts repaired. And as the sun's rays thawed the streams in mountain valleys, they scattered again to begin the quest for beaver that was their life's sole purpose.

To follow this routine successfully year after year—and stay alive—the mountain men had to adjust themselves completely to the wilderness world about them. Their primitive existence revolved about three things: beaver, buffalo, and Indians—or, as they would have phrased it, fur, meat, and ha'r, or their own scalps. To secure fur and meat, they had to risk their ha'r; to keep their ha'r, they had to develop forest skills superior to those of their principal antagonists, the Indians. Of the red men with whom the trappers carried on a constant battle, the Blackfeet of the Three Forks country were most feared; it was understood in the mountains that

[6]William T. Hamilton, *My Sixty Years on the Plains* (New York, 1905), pp. 97–98.
[7]Rufus B. Sage, *Rocky Mountain Life; or, Startling Scenes and Perilous Adventures in the Far West* (Boston, 1859), pp. 348–349.

when a trapper saw a Blackfoot or a Blackfoot saw a trapper, shooting started at once. Yet even such friendly Indians as the Crows could never be completely trusted, for few could resist stealing a carelessly watched horse or pouncing on an unwary white man. Constant vigilance and superb skill were necessary just to stay alive in such a country.

Nature, too, required both strength and ability of those who would survive in the forests and deserts of the West. Wild animals, only scarcely less dangerous than Indians, abounded there. Most feared were the grizzly bears that roamed the Rockies in such numbers that trappers saw as many as fifty or sixty a day. Every step that a mountain man took might bring him face to face with a savage she-grizzly, taller than himself and with great raking claws that could cut to the bone at every sweep, or might be followed by the sudden "whurrr" and strike of a deadly rattlesnake. He was menaced, too, by the numbing cold of mountain winters and by the constant danger of starvation common to all men who gambled with nature for their food. Many a trapper survived a winter blizzard or a summer desert march only by bleeding his horse and drinking the blood, by cutting off and eating the ears of his mule, or by choking down the leather thongs of his moccasins after they had been boiled until soft. One old mountaineer recalled: "I have held my hands in an ant-hill until they were covered with ants, then greedily licked them off. I have taken the soles of my moccasins, crisped them in the fire, and eaten them. In our extremity the large black crickets which are found in the country were considered game. We used to take a kettle of hot water, catch the crickets and throw them in, and when they stopped kicking, eat them."[8]

In such an environment the mountain men could live only by reverting to the primitive themselves. Their wilderness skills had to match those of their savage opponents; their strength and endurance had to be great enough to withstand the ravages of a hostile nature. They had to know instinctively whether the grinning wolf's face that appeared momentarily from behind a clump of cottonwoods was really a Blackfoot in disguise, whether the faint cry of a night bird was actually a Bannock signaling his companions, whether a furtive footfall heard from beyond the campfire was that of a Comanche after their horses. Their lives were a constant vigil against dangers seen and unseen; not for a moment could they relax. "The expression on their countenances," wrote one who knew them well, "is watchful, solemn, and determined. They ride and walk like men whose breasts have so long been exposed to the bullet and the arrow, that fear finds within them no resting place."[9]

Some, in this reversion to the primitive, descended even below the level of the Indian. Edward Rose was such a man; a morose, moody misfit who had fled west after a career as river pirate and outlaw, he became famed for his uncanny skills as a woodsman before joining the Crow Indians and forsaking civilization entirely. A fellow trapper saw Rose lead his tribesmen to victory

[8]Victor, *River of the West*, p. 120.
[9]Thomas J. Farnham, *Travels in the Great Western Prairies, the Anahuac and Rocky Mountains, and in the Oregon Country* (Poughkeepsie, 1841), p. 240.

against a Blackfoot war party in 1834 then whip his followers into a bloody frenzy as they hacked off the hands of the wounded enemy warriors, pierced their bodies with pointed sticks, and plucked out their eyes.[10] Jim Beckwith was another; like Rose, he forsook civilization to join the Crow tribe, and he, too, became a prominent chief.[11] Equally touched by the wand of savagery was Charles Gardner, who borrowed the nickname "Phil" from his native Philadelphia. Sent on a journey with a lone Indian companion, he was given up for lost after a howling winter gale suddenly swept the countryside. To his companions' surprise, Phil reappeared after several days, but without the Indian. As he unpacked his mule, they saw him pull out a black and shriveled human leg, which he threw to the ground with: "There, damn you, I won't have to gnaw on you any more." "Cannibal Phil," as he was known thereafter, added to his unenviable reputation a few years later when, marooned in the mountains by a snowstorm, he subsisted comfortably on the flesh of his current squaw.[12]

Such extremes of savagery were rare among the mountain men, yet all exhibited a skill in coping with their red-skinned foes that marked them as only slightly more advanced in the scale of civilization than Edward Rose or "Cannibal Phil." Their methods of warfare were borrowed from their enemies; they fought as in-

[10]Zenas Leonard, *Adventures of Zenas Leonard, Fur Trader and Trapper, 1831–1836* (Cleveland, 1904), pp. 262–270.

[11]James P. Beckwourth, *The Life and Adventures of James P. Beckwourth* (New York, 1856). On becoming an author, Jim Beckwith adopted this more dignified name.

[12]LeRoy R. Hafen, "Mountain Men: Big Phil the Cannibal," *Colorado Magazine* 13 (March, 1936): 53–58.

dividuals, using brush and rocks for cover and gradually closing with their opponents until they ended in hand-to-hand combat. There they were superb; they had to be to live. They could throw a hunting knife or tomahawk with unerring accuracy or shoot their stubby rifles with a nonchalant skill that took a frightful toll. After one engagement, several mountain men argued over who had killed a particularly gaudily dressed chief. One insisted that they would find his bullet in the chief's left eye; when the body was pulled from the creek where it had fallen, the bullet was exactly in the spot prophesied.[13] When a battle was won, the trappers always scalped their victims as did the Indians, making two semicircular incisions with and against the sun, loosening the skin with the point of the knife, and pulling with both feet planted against the dead warrior's shoulders until the scalp came loose with a characteristic "flop."[14]

Mountain men took as much pride in escaping from their foes as they did in killing them, just as did the Indians, for when surprised or outnumbered they had a chance to display their wilderness skill as they could not in ordinary combat. Typical was the ingenuity shown by one trapper when, returning from a buffalo hunt with his horse laden with meat, he was surprised by three Blackfeet. Dropping the meat, he tried to outrun them, but saw they were gaining steadily. Suddenly he plunged his knife into his horse's neck, severing the spine, so the animal dropped dead instantly. Throwing

    [13]Nolie Mumey, *The Life of Jim Baker, 1818–1898* (Denver, 1931), pp. 32–33.
    [14]Richard F. Burton, *The City of the Saints* (London, 1861), p. 138.

himself behind the carcass, he shot one of his pursuers dead. The other two started to approach from different sides before he could reload, but he killed one with his pistol and the other fled. Taking their ponies, he reloaded the meat he had abandoned and rode calmly into camp.[15]

Another mountain man, hunting on the fringes of the Blackfoot country during the summer of 1835, set out alone one frosty night to explore a stream that was reputed to be rich in beaver. Approaching it with caution, he found beaver sign plentiful and noiselessly set his traps, alert for the slightest sound as he did so. Then he concealed himself and his horse in a thicket and slept until daylight, when he took four skins from his traps before returning to his hiding place to sleep until late afternoon. On awakening, he scanned the landscape for thirty minutes, searching for any movement that would betray an Indian. His vigilance was rewarded, for at the end of that time a Blackfoot warrior emerged from a clump of cottonwoods and stood perfectly still for fifteen minutes surveying the countryside. Satisfied that no one was about, the Indian gave three whistles; from upstream four more Blackfeet appeared. One had six beaver skins; as the trapper watched, they pinned the pelts to the ground to dry then brought in three more skins from their own traps. When the trapper saw four of the Indians leave to hunt, he knew he could escape from the one left on guard, but he stayed hidden, thinking of

15John Dunn, *The Oregon Country, and the British North American Fur Trade* (Philadelphia, 1845), pp. 223–224; John K. Townsend, *Narrative of a Journey Across the Rocky Mountains to the Columbia River* (Philadelphia, 1839), pp. 222–223.

those nine beaver skins. His opportunity came when the sound of shots signaled the success of the hunting party. The guard hurried away at once; the trapper slipped from his thicket, rolled up the nine beaver skins, and rode into camp that night with thirteen skins and his own scalp.[16]

One of the most remarkable escapes in which a mountain man surpassed the red men in their own skills was that of John Colter. With a companion named Potts, Colter was paddling down the Jefferson River when he rounded a bend to find himself in a camp of eight hundred Blackfeet. There was no chance of escape; instead, Colter quietly slid his traps overboard to save them and paddled ashore, hoping that he would only be robbed. His companion, however, refused to land. From his canoe he killed one of the Indians with a rifle shot. That was Potts's death warrant. His body was riddled with arrows, dragged ashore, and hacked to pieces, and the entrails were thrown in Colter's face. Colter knew that his own death was certain now; friends of the Indian killed by Potts threatened him with knives and tomahawks. Instead, the chiefs held a council. When it was over they motioned for him to take off his clothes, then said in the Crow language: "Go, go away." Colter walked slowly from the camp, expecting to be shot in the back at any moment. When he had gone a hundred yards he turned to see the younger warriors throwing off their outer garments. Now he knew his fate: he was to be the prize in a race for life, with his scalp going to the winner.

16Marsh, *Four Years in the Rockies*, pp. 131–132.

Colter ran now, across an open plain where sage-brush raked his legs and the cruel needles of the prickly pear pierced his bare feet. Five miles ahead, he knew, lay the Madison River, where he could find shelter and might possibly escape. Halfway there, and with blood gushing from his nose and mouth, he paused to look back. One warrior was almost upon him; the rest were far back. Colter pleaded for his life in the Crow tongue, but the Blackfoot only leveled his spear and charged. With a superhuman effort, Colter grabbed the spear and twisted it so violently that it broke, throwing the Indian to the ground. Now it was the Indian's turn to plead for his life, but Colter killed him with his own spearpoint, took his blanket, and ran on with some hope of escape. Reaching the Madison River with his pursuers some distance behind, he concealed himself so skillfully that they searched for him in vain for the rest of the day. That night he climbed the mountains that fringed the Madison Valley and set out on foot for his companions' camp, three hundred miles away. Eleven days later, his bare limbs and feet swollen and torn, his thin body so emaciated that he was unrecognizable, he joined his friends. Here, indeed, was a feat of frontier skill of which an Indian could have been proud.[17]

Such spectacular exploits demonstrated the mountain men's reversion to savagery no more effectively than

[17]The two contemporary accounts of Colter's "race for life" are in John Bradbury, *Travels in the Interior of America* (London, 1817), pp. 18–21, and Thomas James, *Three Years Among the Indians and Mexicans* (St. Louis, 1915), pp. 57–64. James was with Colter when he retraced the route of his run some years later. The story is also told in detail in Burton Harris, *John Colter: His Years in the Rockies* (New York, 1952), and Stallo Vinton, *John Colter, Discoverer of Yellowstone Park* (New York, 1926).

did their less spectacular day-by-day life in the West. In that life, as in their warfare with the Indians, experience taught them that they could survive only by adopting the customs perfected by the red men in generations of adjustment to wilderness living. They must revert to a state of semisavagery, yet retain enough of their higher civilization to be superior to their enemies. This adjustment was made by all successful mountain men; those who failed did not live to tell the tale. In the clothes they wore, the food they ate, the language they spoke, and even the mental attitudes they embraced, the trappers showed their ability to descend centuries in the scale of civilization within a few months or years.

Certainly in appearance there was little to distinguish the mountain men from their foes. Gaunt and spare, with skin tanned the color of the Indian's by life in the open, unkempt hair hanging to their shoulders, and grizzled beards "that would scarcely disgrace the Bedouin of the desert,"[18] they usually wore a hunting shirt of buckskin decorated at every seam with rows of colored porcupine quills or long leather thongs, pantaloons that were similarly ornamented, leather moccasins, and a hat of beaver or otter skin. Over their left shoulders hung a powder horn and a bullet pouch; a large butcher knife and sometimes a pistol and tomahawk projected from a leather belt worn around the waist, and a "possibles" sack containing a pipe, tobacco, gun wiper, and bullet mold dangled at their sides.[19]

[18]Townsend, *Narrative of a Journey*, p. 176.
[19]Contemporary descriptions of the dress of the mountain men are in Ruxton, *Adventures in Mexico and the Rocky Mountains*, p. 243; Sage, *Rocky Mountain Life*, p. 38; Pike, *Prose Sketches and Poems*,

Romantic though these clothes might be, they could best be appreciated at a distance, for like the Indians that they imitated, the mountain men seldom washed their garments from the day they were donned to the day they were discarded.[20] At their sides they carried a short-barreled, large-caliber rifle that fired a heavy lead bullet with such terrific energy that it would bring down a buffalo at two hundred yards.[21] With this rifle in the crook of his arm, a six-shooter revolver in his belt, and knife and tomahawk ready to throw with deadly accuracy, the mountain man was a regular walking arsenal.

Because they knew that their lives depended on flight as often as combat, the trappers paid as much attention to their horses as did the Indians. The tough, fleet, wiry little ponies that they rode were obtained by barter or theft, as was the practice among the red men; occasionally a wild horse would be captured by "creasing" its neck—firing a single bullet so accurately that it grazed the neck bone and stunned the horse for a few moments.[22] The usual mountain man also owned a mule or two for use as pack animals. Not only did these tough little beasts show greater endurance than a horse in desert country, but trappers insisted that mules were the

p. 38; Russell, *Journal of a Trapper*, p. 85; A. Adolphus Wislizenus, *A Journey to the Rocky Mountains in the Year 1839* (St. Louis, 1912), pp. 86–87; and J. N. B. Hewitt, ed., *Journal of Randolph Friederich Kurz* (Washington, D.C., 1937), p. 30.

20P. L. Edwards, "Rocky Mountain Correspondence from the Missouri Enquirer," *Niles' Register* 47 (October 11, 1834): 92.

21Chauncey Thomas, "Frontier Firearms," *Colorado Magazine* 7 (May, 1930): 102–103.

22John B. Wyeth, *Oregon; or, A Short History of a Long Journey* (Cambridge, Mass., 1833), p. 87.

natural enemies of the Indians and would raise their ears, snort, and stare toward approaching red men long before a horse or man could sense their coming.[23] Beasts that could give such a warning often saved trappers' lives. Thus equipped with his horse, a pack mule carrying his trap sack and blankets, a Hawken rifle, and a hunting knife, the mountain man could live handsomely without further help from man.

The buffalo was his staff of life, just as it was the Indian's. During the winter when only scrawny bulls were available, the trappers grew thin and scrawny themselves; in the spring, as the cows grew sleek and fat so did the mountain men.[24] These great shaggy beasts were everywhere on the plains that fringed the Rockies and in the mountain valleys themselves, so numerous that as far as the eye could see their brown bodies dotted the landscape—"a vast expanse of moving, plunging, rolling, rushing life—a literal sea of dark forms," as one awe-struck traveler wrote.[25] Here was food for the taking. A trapper had only to gallop his horse into a herd, single out the fat buffalo cow that he wanted, and ride beside the slow-moving beast until a well-planted rifle bullet brought it down to assure himself a feast fit for a king.[26]

A savage king, that is, for even the eating habits of the mountain men paralleled those of the Indians. A

[23]Edwin L. Sabin, *Kit Carson Days* (New York, 1935), I, 98–102.
[24]Warren A. Ferris, *Life in the Rocky Mountains, 1830–1835* (Salt Lake City, 1940), p. 39.
[25]Ibid., p. 27.
[26]Marsh, *Four Years in the Rockies*, pp. 94–95; E. Willard Smith, "Journal of E. Willard Smith while with the Fur Traders, Vasquez and Sublette, in the Rocky Mountain Region, 1839–1840," *Oregon Historical Quarterly* 14 (September, 1913): 256–257.

trapper began preparing a meal by propping row on row of juicy hump ribs about a fire of buffalo chips—the sun-dried dung of the buffalo that was the universal fuel of the West. While the ribs were sizzling, he often began his meal by drinking some of the warm blood, which he insisted tasted like milk.[27] This might be followed by the buffalo liver, eaten raw and flavored with the contents of the gall bladder, or by a soup made from a pound or two of rich marrow extracted from the leg bones and cooked with blood and water. This thick mixture turned the stomachs of easterners but made the faces of trappers "shine with grease and gladness."[28] The intestines were eaten next, roasted until they were puffed with heat and fat and sizzling with escaping steam. These "boudins" the men slid down their throats without chewing; on occasion two trappers would start on the opposite ends of a great pile of intestines and work their way to the middle, each eating faster and faster to get his share and shouting to the other to "feed fair."[29] Then came the main course of hump ribs. Rib after rib was torn from its place and the chunks of meat gulped down as the rich fat dripped over the mountain man's face and clothing.

How they did eat when hunting was good, for like the Indians or wild animals they never knew when their next meal would come—if ever. "When we have a plenty," wrote one mountaineer, "we eat the best pieces first, for fear of being killed by some brat of an Indian

[27]James, *Three Years Among the Indians and Mexicans*, p. 116.
[28]Farnham, *Travels in the Great Western Prairies*, p. 203.
[29]Ruxton, *Adventures in Mexico and the Rocky Mountains*, pp. 267–268; Lewis H. Garrard, *Wah-to-Yah and the Taos Trail* (Cincinnati, 1850), p. 26.

before we have enjoyed them."[30] Eight or nine pounds of meat a day was normal for a robust trapper. "We rise in the morning with the sun," wrote a traveler with a trapping party, "stir up our fires, and *roast* our breakfast, usually eating from one to two pounds of meat at a morning meal. At ten o'clock we lunch, dine at two, sup at five, and lunch at eight, and during the night-watch commonly provide ourselves with two or three 'hump-ribs' and a marrow bone, to furnish enjoyment and keep the drowsy god at a distance."[31] Occasionally they would add deer or elk or bear meat to their diet; in the spring they nibbled at the roots of the white apple and the commote; in the summer wild cherries and berries were eaten greedily.[32] But these variations were not necessary. Buffalo was all they needed. "We live upon it solely," one wrote, "without bread or vegetables of any kind, and what seems most singular, we never tire of or disrelish it."[33] Indeed, to the mountain man the meat of a fat cow buffalo was not only food and drink but a cure for all the body's ills. It would, one solemnly declared, "cure dyspepsy, prevent consumption, amend a broken constitution, put flesh on the bones of a *skeleton,* and *restore a dead man* to life."[34] Eating habits scarcely distinguishable from those of wild animals again reflected the reversion to the primitive that was taking place.

In their speech as well, the mountain men showed the persuasive influence of their environment. They

[30]Farnham, *Travels in the Great Western Prairies,* p. 202.
[31]Townsend, *Narrative of a Journey,* p. 216.
[32]Sage, *Rocky Mountain Life,* p. 147.
[33]Ferris, *Life in the Rocky Mountains,* p. 39.
[34]Sage, *Rocky Mountain Life,* pp. 69, 71.

spoke in high-pitched voices, emphasizing each word as did the Indians whose dialects they heard more frequently than their native tongue. They gestured frequently and meaningfully as they talked, for intertribal communication among the Indians was in the sign language, and at that the trappers were adept. From the red men, too, they borrowed many words and expressions as well as the colorful imagery normally used in the Indians' speech. French and Mexican trappers with whom they were in constant contact contributed to the mountain men's language; the frontiersmen also borrowed words from the artifacts that they used and from the world of nature about them. The result was a language as unique as the clothes that they wore or the food that they ate and as admirably adjusted to the primitive environment of the West. The red men of the forest could understand them more readily than could the families they had left behind in New York or London.

The imagery that was the most distinguishing feature of the trappers' speech came largely from Indian dialects. A man was a "child" or a "hoss" or a "coon" or a "nigger." A hungry man was "wolfish" and needed to fill his "meatbag" with good "buffler meat" or "cow meat"; one who was thirsty drank to satisfy his "dry."[35] "Well, hos!" said one old mountaineer while glorifying the virtues of dog meat as food, "I'll dock off the buffler, and then if thar's any meat that runs can take the shine outen dog, you can slide."[36] To scalp an Indian was to "lift his ha'r" or "tickle his fleece"; one who had been

35Hamilton, *My Sixty Years on the Plains*, p. 31.
36Garrard, *Wah-to-Yah and the Taos Trail*, p. 47.

killed was "rubbed out" or had "gone under."[37] Phrases such as "hyar's a nigger lifted ha'r that spree" were sprinkled through their conversation. Winter to the mountain men was "robe season" or "freezin' time." Said one who rose early on a winter morning: "This hos is no ba'r to stick his nose under cover all robe season."[38] To get something free was to have it "on the prairie." "How are ye off for cow meat?" one trapper asked another when they met in the Rockies one winter. "Hell!" said the other, "Cow meat *this* freezin' time? You've bin down to Santa Fee too long. Why, poor bull is hard to get. . . . Howsomever, if you want to chaw on lean buffler dryed, you can have it on the prairie."[39] Nor could a mountain man utter more than a few words without injecting the "Wah" or "Ugh" or "Heap" of the red men.

From the implements and customs of his unusual life he also adopted words and phrases that were unintelligible to Easterners. Gunpowder was "Du Pont" from its makers, bullets were "Galenas" from the lead mines around that Illinois town, and knives were "Green Rivers" from the trademark of the most common make. To "stick a Bug Boy up to the Green River" meant to plunge a knife into a Blackfoot Indian as far as the trademark high on its blade.[40] A beaver skin was a "plew," while a person doomed to die was a "gone beaver." Instead of saying "if that is what you mean,"

37Sage, *Rocky Mountain Life*, p. 119; Ruxton, *Adventures in Mexico and the Rocky Mountains*, p. 273; Ruxton, *Life in the Far West*, p. 4.
38Garrard, *Wah-to-Yah and the Taos Trail*, p. 185.
39Ibid., p. 117.
40Ibid., pp. 185–186.

a trapper would commonly remark "if that's the way your stick floats," referring to the stick that floated over each beaver trap to mark its position. Said one old trapper, when asked during a visit to the East whether he had traveled widely: "A sight, marm, this coon's gone over, if that's the way your stick floats. I've trapped beaver on Platte and Arkansa, and away up Missoura and Yeller Stone; I've trapped on Columbia, on Lewis Fork, and Green River; I've trapped, marm, on Grand River and the Heely. I've fout the Blackfoot (and d--d bad Injuns they are); I've raised hair on more than one Apach, and made a Rapaho come afore now; I've trapped in Heav'n, in airth, and h—."[41]

The French and Spanish traders who invaded the Rockies from Canada and Mexico also contributed colorful words to the language of the trappers. When danger threatened, a mountain man would instinctively call out "Lave ho! Lave!" without realizing that he was using the corruption of the Spanish word *levar*.[42] The French term *cache* was used as a synonym for "hide."[43] "Do 'ee hyar now, boys," said one old trapper on seeing traces left by Indians, "thar's sign about. This old hoss feels like caching."[43] To perform an act of bravery was to "count coup." Liquor to a mountain man was "Taos lightning" from a fiery fluid produced in that Mexican town, or sometimes "Picketwire firewater" from his corruption of the name of the Purgatoire River. Any dance was a "fandango," while fancy clothes were "fofarraw." On the southwestern frontier especially, trappers

41Ruxton, *Life in the Far West*, pp. 7–8.
42Sage, *Rocky Mountain Life*, p. 58.
43Ruxton, *Life in the Far West*, p. 114.

spiced their speech with such words; a traveler there met one who "*sacre-ed* in French, *caraho-ed* in Spanish-Mexican, interpolated *thunder strike you* in Cheyenne, or . . . genuinely and emphatically *damned* in American."[44]

The mountain man blended the imagery of the Indian, phrases borrowed from his own experience, and the explosive epithets of his neighbors into a language that was both colorful and expressive. He spoke seldom and in compact phrases; men who live much alone waste few words. Two trappers meeting in the West had this conversation:

"What's the sign?"

"Pawnees."

"How'd they number, and which way?"

"Twenty odd, and toward the sothe."

"Arter hair?"

"I reckon."

"Be apt to trouble us?"

"Think they passed with thar eyes shut?"

"Playing possum, maybe. How long gone?"

"Less nor a quarter."

". . . Spect we'd better put out and look for camp?"

"I reckon."

"Augh."[45]

Only when the trappers relaxed about the campfire or lounged lazily in winter camp did their speech flow freely. Then they loved to spin tales of their battles with Indians or their fights with grizzly bears. A traveler overheard a mountain man reminiscing over one

---

[44]Garrard, *Wah-to-Yah and the Taos Trail*, p. 69.
[45]Emerson Bennett, *The Prairie Flower* (Cincinnati, 1849), p. 44.

brush with the redskins: "They come mighty nigh rubbin' me out, 'tother side of Spanish Peaks—woke up in the mornin' jist afore day, the devils yellin' like mad. I grabs my knife, keels one, an' made for timber with four or five of their cussed arrows in my meatbag. The Paches took my beaver—five packs of the prettiest in the mountains—an' two mules, but my traps was hid in the creek. Sez I, hyar's a gone coon if they keep my gun, so I follows thar trail, an' at night, crawls into camp, an' sock my big knife up to the Green River, first dig. I takes t'other Injun by the har, and makes meat of him, *too*. *Maybe* thar wasn't coups counted, an' a big dance on hand, ef I was alone."[46]

If the speech of the mountain man showed his reversion to the primitive, so also did the mental attitudes that he developed in his lonely wilderness life. The trapper not only lived and talked as did his red-skinned enemies; he even thought as they did. Like the Indian, he placed but slight value on his own life or on the lives of his friends. Death was so commonplace in a land where danger lurked at every turn that there was no mourning for the dead in the mountains; when a mountaineer heard that a friend had been killed he would shrug his shoulders and say, "Poor fellow! out of luck."[47] Joe Meek, a famous trapper, was hunting buffalo when one of the party was thrown from his horse amidst the trampling herd. Joe was told to ride to his friend's rescue.

"What'll I do with him if he is dead?" he asked.

"Can't you pack him into camp?"

46Garrad, *Wah-to-Yah and the Taos Trail*, pp. 187–188.
47Victor, *River of the West*, p. 59.

"Pack hell," Joe objected, "I would rather pack a load of meat."[48] There was nothing disrespectful or unusual in that remark. Joe only reflected an attitude normal among men who live in constant danger. "Live men was what we wanted," he explained to a friend later; "dead ones was of no account."[49]

Holding his own life in little regard, the mountain man had even less respect for the lives of his foes. Like the Indians, he looked upon every red-skinned stranger as a potential enemy, to be killed first and questioned later. This was a common-sense rule to follow among Indians, but in following it the trapper showed how completely he had reverted to their lower civilization. Thus, on one occasion a band of mountain men were trapping along the Snake River when the alarm of "Injuns!" was sounded. All grabbed their rifles, and a hurried cry of "Shoot!, Shoot!" rang out. The leader checked this "precipitation," ordering the men to hold their fire until the red men approached. The Indians were found to be friendly Crows wanting to trade a few furs for tobacco.[50] On another occasion a trapper killed one of the despised "Digger" Indians of Utah while hunting along the Humboldt River.

"Why did you shoot him?" asked the leader of the party.

"To keep him from stealing my traps."

"Had he stolen any?"

"No; but he looked as if he was going to."[51]

48Sabin, *Kit Carson Days*, I, 180.
49Washington Irving, *The Adventures of Captain Bonneville, U.S.A.* (New York, 1849), p. 95.
50Victor, *River of the West*, p. 80.
51Ibid., p. 122.

No Indian could have acted with more calloused indifference to the value of human life.

Even more typical of the savagery of the mountain men was their cruelty. Instances of captured enemies being put to death by torture are nonexistent, but to that point the trappers displayed the same heartless inhumanity toward their foes that was exhibited by the Indians. Thus, on one occasion a few Blackfeet were surprised while stealing horses. They ran and were chased by the yelling trappers into a dense, dry thicket. The thicket was cold-bloodedly set on fire while the mountain men settled down to shoot those trying to escape and watch the rest burn to death. One disappointed white man wrote that night, "As they were all more or less roasted, we took no scalps."[52] Even when enemies were spared in battle, the motive was seldom humanitarian. In one brush with the Blackfeet, all but one of the natives was killed. A young trapper was about to pick him off when a grizzled old mountain man knocked the gun aside, saying: "Ef ye kill that Injun ye'll do it over my carcase. I want that red varmint to live so's he kin drag into his village an' tell the rest o' them skunks jes' who 'twas rubbed out their war party. Otherwise they might never know. They gotta larn t'respec' decent Christians."[53]

From the Indians, too, the mountain man borrowed both his religious concepts and his whole philosophy

---

[52]Beckwourth, *Life and Adventures of James P. Beckwourth*, p. 80.

[53]Quoted in Frederic E. Voelker, "The Mountain Men and Their Part in the Opening of the West," *Bulletin of the Missouri Historical Society* 3 (August, 1947): 157–158.

of life and death. Christianity in any orthodox sense was unknown in the mountains; according to a classic saying among frontiersmen, there was no Sabbath west of the Missouri. Instead, the trapper who felt any religious impulse took unto himself the gods and practices of the red men. The transition was well demonstrated by one of the most famous of the mountain men, Old Bill Williams. Devoutly religious, Old Bill went west first as a missionary, but he soon succumbed to the lure of the wilderness, married a squaw, and traded his Bible for beaver traps. With a passion for loneliness and solitudes, he spent his life deep in the mountains, where he had an uncanny skill in locating virgin beaver streams and a phenomenal reputation for his roaring sprees at rendezvous time. Yet he remained deeply mystical, brooding much over his fate in afterlife. Gradually he convinced himself that he would return to earth as an elk that would live in a sheltered valley of which he was particularly fond; often he told his companions not to shoot such an elk after his death.[54] In this belief Old Bill only slightly exaggerated the transition that occured in his contemporaries. So completely did they embrace the wilderness way of life that even their basic beliefs reflected savagery rather than civilization.

And like the Indians that they imitated and dispised, the mountain men could find happiness only far from the haunts of men. Passionately fond of the lonely solitudes of the West, they were more at home following a rippling beaver stream in the depths of the Rockies or

[54]Chauncey P. Williams, *Lone Elk: The Life Story of Bill Williams, Trapper and Guide of the Far West* (Denver, 1936), p. 12.

plodding across the alkaline wastes of a parched desert than in the villages of the Mississippi Valley. This was their land, their home. Later comers found the ashes of their campfires scattered over all the West, from the pine forests of the Three Forks country, where they defied the deadly Blackfeet, to the sun-dried canyons of the Colorado, where they braved the wrath of Apaches and Navahos in their endless search for beaver peltry. They could no more leave this lonely land than could the Indians. Old Bill Williams tried to give up trapping once, buying a store in Taos and settling down to haggle over prices with Mexican women. For a few weeks he endured this strange new way of life, then one morning he pitched his whole stock of goods on the street, shouting to the crowd that gathered: "Here, damn you, if I can't sell you goods, I will give them to you." When he tired of watching the women scramble for bolts of calico, he shouldered his rifle and started for the mountains again.[55]

Old Bill in his hatred of civilization typified his fellow trappers. They realized this in the middle 1840's when the extermination of the beaver and a declining market caused by changing European hat styles ended trapping. Gradually the mountain men drifted away, some to work at Santa Fe or Bent's Fort, some to farms in the new lands of Oregon or California, some to lonely cabins in mountain valleys where they could dream of the past, some to the half-forgotten villages of the East where they had spent their early years. Wherever they

[55]Alpheus H. Favour, *Old Bill Williams, Mountain Man* (Chapel Hill, N.C., 1936), pp. 73–74.

went beyond the mountains they found life strange and terrifying and uncomfortable. A friend visited one in his California home and listened to his complaint: "Living upon bacon, bread, milk and sich like mushy stuff ... don't agree with me," the old man whined; "it never will agree with a man of my age, eighty-three last—. ... I thought I would take a small hunt, to get a little exercise for my old bones, and some good fresh meat. The grisly bear, fat deer, and poultry, and fish—them are such things as a man should eat."[56] Three years later, as a hunting party passed his door, the mountain man could still sing out, "Be sure, boys, and bring me back a squaw."[57] Another who tried life in Missouri voiced the same complaint: "It's hard to fetch breath amongst them big bands of corncrackers of Missoura. Beside, it goes against natur to leave buffler meat and feed on hog; and them white gals are too much like picturs, and a deal too 'fofarrow.' No; darn the settlements, I say."[58]

There spoke men who had not only abandoned but also renounced civilization. In their reversion to the primitive they typified the process that transformed every frontiersman as he drifted westward, whether trapper, cattleman, miner, or pioneer farmer. All succumbed to the wilderness world in which they found themselves, and all were forced with the passing years to begin the climb upward to civilization once more. Little wonder that in this recurring process the chains

[56]Edwin Bryant, *What I Saw in California* (New York, 1848), p. 355.
[57]Theodore T. Johnson, *Sights in the Gold Region, and Scenes by the Way* (New York, 1849), pp. 171–173.
[58]Ruxton, *Life in the Far West*, p. 18.

of tradition were weakened. Little wonder that in this constant rebirth of society over the course of three centuries there emerged in America a race differing from that of England—a race whose roots were in the past but whose characteristics and institutions had been modified by an all-powerful nature that had reshaped its conquerors even in the midst of their conquest.

# The Frontier and
# American Culture

Historians of America's frontiering experience have
long accepted a plausible explanation of the manner in
which pioneering altered men and their institutions. As
settlers moved westward, they say, the garments of civilization were discarded. Some were shed as superfluous
during the journey. Others were cast aside as the frontiersmen grappled with raw nature in their new homes;
to subdue the wilderness they had to revert to a state
of near savagery, abandoning cultural pursuits and social organization while they planted the first seeds of
civilization. Then—so the story goes—the influx of newcomers and the corresponding thickening of population
made possible a gradual ascent from primitivism. Eventually a fully matured social order emerged. This differed from its counterparts in the Old World or the

Delivered as the Edith Coulter Lecture before the California
Library Association on November 5, 1964, and published by the Association as Keepsake Number 7 in 1965. Made possible by a faculty
research grant from the Social Science Research Council in 1959–1960
and by a grant-in-aid from the Huntington Library and Art Gallery
in the summer of 1960.

[51]

East, for the unique environment, the acculturation inevitable as people from differing backgrounds met and mingled, and the accidental deviations normal in the evolution of isolated societies all contributed to the distinctiveness of frontier communities. They, in turn, merged to create an American civilization different from that of Europe.

This explanation is both compact and convincing. But does it mirror normal human behavior? Can man discard his cultural heritage overnight, reverting to a state of near savagery on contact with the wilderness? Or does he, as a product of a centuries-old culture, cling to his heritage and resist the eroding influences of a primitive environment? These are questions well worth examining if we are to understand the American past in particular and man's behavior in general.

That some pioneers seized the opportunity to secede from civilization in certainly true. Travelers journeying westward in the eighteenth and nineteenth centuries were conscious of a cultural fault as observable as a geological fault when they entered frontier areas; "everything and everybody," wrote one, ". . . looks wild and half savage."[1] Even in the seventeenth century a visitor to the Swedish settlements on the Delaware River found the transplanted Europeans "not much better than savages," and given to fighting, drunkenness, and laziness;[2] a hundred years later a minister in the Carolina backwoods was rudely told that the settlers wanted "no D--d Black Gown Sons of Bitches among them" to

---

1William Faux, *Memorable Days in America* (London, 1823), p. 206.

2Peter Kalm, *Travels into North America* (London, 1772), II, 711.

[52]

interfere with their constant "Revelling, Drinking, Singing, Dancing, and Whoring." On that frontier, he reported sadly, "many hund[reds] do live in Concumbinage, swopping their wives as Cattel, and living in a State of Nature, more irregularly and unchastely than the Indians."[3]

As the frontier swept westward across the Appalachians, the thermometer of sin rose steadily. In early Kentucky and Tennessee fights were common with no holds barred and each antagonist seeking to maim his opponent by biting off his nose or gouging out an eye. Kentucky's legislature in 1798 enacted special penalties for slitting a nose or ear or pulling out an eye while fighting.[4] A traveler visiting a Nashville jail in the 1830's found three prisoners: one confined for gouging, one for stabbing, and one for biting off an enemy's nose.[5] Popular in the West was the tale of a well-known gouger who, after conversion at a camp meeting, wrestled with the Devil on the mourners' bench while his friends shouted, "Gouge him, Billy! gouge him, Billy! gouge him!"[6] Ralph Waldo Emerson may have had such

[3]Charles Woodmason, *The Carolina Backcountry on the Eve of the Revolution: The Journal and Other Writings of Charles Woodmason, Anglican Itinerant*, ed. Richard J. Hooker (Chapel Hill, N.C., 1953), pp. 15–17.

[4]Quoted in Ralph Rusk, *The Literature of the Middle Western Frontier* (New York, 1925), I, 75.

[5]James E. Alexander, *Transatlantic Sketches, Comprising Visits to the Most Interesting Scenes in North and South America and the West Indies* (London, 1833), II, 107.

[6]Baynard Rush Hall, *The New Purchase; or, Seven and a Half Years in the Far West* (New York, 1843), II, 158–159. Eye-gouging stories, some of which may be believed, are common in the travel literature of the time. For typical accounts, see Thomas Ashe, *Travels in America, Performed in 1806* (London, 1808), I, 225–231; Fortescue Cuming, *Sketches of a Tour to the Western Country* (Pittsburgh, 1810),

episodes in mind when he wrote, "The pioneers are commonly the off-scourings of civilized society."[7]

The frontier was an area of depressed moral standards and relatively uninhibited social conduct, but the frontier was not, despite Emerson's dictum, inhabited solely by profane, tobacco-spitting, nose-biting, eye-gouging, half-horse-and-half-alligator riproarers. This distortion has been inflicted on modern scholarship by two contemporary misconceptions. One was the belief that a few pockets of lawlessness—the Mississippi river towns, the annual rendezvous of the mountain men, the cattle towns and mining camps, the "hells on wheels" that housed the railroad work crews—typified frontier living. Despite their attraction to travelers, who described them endlessly, these backwashes were peopled by only a handful of the thousands of pioneers who won the West. The long shadow that they have cast over American legend is far out of proportion to their importance.

pp. 118–119; Simon A. O'Ferrall, *A Ramble of Six Thousand Miles through the United States of America* (London, 1832), pp. 169–170; and Charles Sealsfield, *The Americans As They Are, Described in a Tour through the Valley of the Mississippi* (London, 1828), pp. 23–27. Colorful, but sketchy, information is in Robert V. Haynes, "Law Enforcement in Frontier Mississippi," *Journal of Mississippi History* 22 (January, 1960): 41–42.

7Quoted in Ernest Marchand, "Emerson and the Frontier," *American Literature* 3 (May, 1931): 154–155. In justice to the pioneers, it must be pointed out that British travelers especially exaggerated frontier violence because they saw what they wanted to see. Those with anti-American prejudices encountered in the West a savage land; those with opposite views found peace and civilization. One traveler noted that if Americans recorded their impressions of England against a similar background of bias, "they would be singling out not the best nor the average, but the worst classes of the population," and could, if they wished, provide "a very harrowing calendar of crime." William A. Baillie-Grohman, *Camps in the Rockies* (New York, 1882), p. 27.

Just as destructive of truth was the failure of western travelers, and even of some westerners, to distinguish between the "backwoodsmen" or "squatters" and the small-farmers who made up the bulk of the frontiersmen. The squatters were maladjusted discontents who frequented the most advanced frontiers. Compulsive seceders from society, they fled into the forest depths, clearing the first fields, building the first crude huts, and dividing their time between hunting and farming. Neighbors they could not abide; the sound of an ax nearby would only send them deeper into the wilderness. Their lives were spent in sloth, indolence, and ignorance; they were sworn enemies of all culture and all learning. Today their counterparts can be found in the asphalt jungles of the cities. Yet like the rivermen and mountain men, the squatters attracted the interest of visitors, who described them so glowingly that both contemporaries and later historians were misled into picturing them as the true pioneers in the conquest of the West.[8]

[8]The growth of legend concerning frontier lawlessness, and the different patterns of growth needed to please differing audiences, is learnedly and amusingly described in Kent L. Steckmesser, *The Western Hero in History and Legend* (Norman, Okla., 1965). Social psychologists detect normal behavior patterns in the men who helped create a tradition of a "Wild West." All persons, they say, are self-centered with an urge to do what they please regardless of consequences. The great majority, however, are restrained by the habits and regulations of society, which shape conduct along lines necessary for group living. When these restraints are removed, as they were on the outer fringes of the frontier, an anarchistic social situation almost inevitably follows, with an almost instinctive return to antisocial behavior. A classic treatment of this subject is in William I. Thomas and Florian Znaniecki, *The Polish Peasant in Europe and America* (New York, 1927), II, 1647–1652, which describes the effects of change of environment on individuals.

Nothing could be further from the truth. The West was won not by swaggering reprobates or indolent backwoodsmen, but by the thousands of small-propertied farmers, ranchers, and entrepreneurs who formed the bulk of the westward-moving population. They came west to stay and grow up with the country. Most had had some pioneering experience; all had some wealth, for the frontier was no place for the penniless. In their new homes a few succumbed to the vagrant habits of the squatters and began the drifting that predestined failure, but far more persisted until neighbors thickened about them and the transition to civilization began. These were America's true frontiersmen, both in numbers and in impact. If we are to understand the frontier process, we must ask whether they succumbed to barbarism or perpetuated the culture they had known in the East.

The answer to that question is not simple. Most were men of small learning, ill-equipped by training to serve as mediums for the transplanting of civilization. Yet nearly all were determined to transfer the cultural institutions of their homelands to their new communities. Some could do so, for nearly every pioneer settlement contained an educated group which assumed leadership functions. The will and the way were both present, yet the ambitions were to be partially unfulfilled, for social and economic conditions on the frontier doomed all efforts to build in the West patent-office models of eastern civilization. Both these environmental conditions and the determination of the pioneers to duplicate accustomed patterns help explain the unique western culture that did emerge.

The urge was there. Wrote Henry Ward Beecher as he watched the westward-flowing tide in the 1850's: "They drive schools along with them as shepherds drive flocks. They have herds of churches, academies, lyceums; and their religious and educational institutions go lowing along the western plains as Jacob's herds lowed along the Syrian hills."[9] So slavishly did they imitate eastern life that some of their villages could scarcely be distinguished from those they left behind. "Were I," a traveler noted, "to drop, like Cyrano from the moon, and to land, unlike Cyrano, in Painesville, Ohio, I would immediately inquire for the Boston and Albany station. There are the same drooping elms, the same pilastered houses, the same Common, the same noble church, as in lovely Massachusetts."[10] A housewife on a Kansas homestead summed up the dreams of the pioneers when she reminisced: "I have read in books that the people of the frontier kept moving ever westward to escape civilization. But if my experience counts for anything, such people were the exceptions. So eager were we to keep in touch with civilization that even when we could not afford a shot gun and ammunition to kill rabbits, we subscribed to newspapers and periodicals and bought books."[11]

9Quoted in Dixon Wecter, "Instruments of Culture on the Frontier," *Yale Review* 36 (Winter, 1947): 246.
10Rollin L. Hartt, "The Ohioans," *Atlantic Monthly* 84 (November, 1899): 682.
11Elise D. Isely, *Sunbonnet Days* (Caldwell, Idaho, 1935), p. 180. The best case for the thesis that eastern civilization advanced almost unchanged into the wilderness has been made by Louis B. Wright, "The Westward Advance of the Atlantic Frontier," *Huntington Library Quarterly* 11 (May, 1948): 261–275, and *Culture on the Moving Frontier* (Bloomington, Ind., 1955). Briefer explorations of this theme are in

These ambitions were often realized. The records of New Salem, Illinois, where Abraham Lincoln whetted his taste for learning, show that all frontier hamlets were not cultural deserts. New Salem in 1832 was only three years old and boasted only 150 inhabitants, but it supported a good subscription school, a flourishing debating society, a temperance society, a nonsectarian Sunday school, and several respectable private libraries whose owners cheerfully loaned books. Much has been said of the fact that young Lincoln had to borrow books, but less of the equally significant fact that books were on hand to be borrowed. The future president was able to thumb the pages of Shakespeare and Robert Burns, to study Kirkham's *Grammar* and the six books of Euclid, and to read Paine and Volney and Jefferson as well as newspapers and periodicals. Yet New Salem flourished for only six years and was a ghost town in ten.[12]

A similar story, on a grander scale, can be told of Lexington, Kentucky, which in 1810, with a population of only four thousand persons, was proclaimed the "Athens of the West." There, two bookstores dispensed learning, three academies flourished, and Transylvania University attracted students even from the East by its rich intellectual fare. This atmosphere attracted writers,

Howard Mumford Jones, *America and French Culture, 1750–1848* (Chapel Hill, N.C., 1927), pp. 50–51, and Earl Pomeroy, "Toward a Reorientation of Western History: Continuity and Environment," *Mississippi Valley Historical Review* 41 (March, 1955): 582–583, 591–592.

12Benjamin Thomas, *Lincoln's New Salem* (Springfield, Ill., 1934), pp. 29–36.

editors, architects, and even painters. Within a few years Lexington boasted a theater, a natural history museum, reading rooms, a remarkably good magazine called the *Western Review*, and its own school of painting under Mathew Jouett. There in 1817 was given the first performance of a Beethoven symphony in the United States.[13] That this record was not entirely unique was shown when a citizen in nearby Cincinnati, plagued by the excessive demands of the village's cultural life, wrote feelingly: "twenty sermons a week—, Sunday evening Discourses on Theology—private assemblies—state Cotillion parties—Saturday Night Clubs, and chemical lectures . . . like the fever and the ague, return every day with distressing regularity."[14]

So persuasive was the urge to perpetuate eastern civilization that even the most primitive frontiersmen sometimes succumbed. The half-savage mountain men, loafing through the cold months in their lonely winter camps, read avidly whenever books were available; one trapper recalled reading during one winter from Byron, Shakespeare, and Scott in addition to the Bible and Clark's commentary on the Scriptures, as well as "other small works in Geology, chemistry and philosophy." Another confessed that he had learned much from the

---

13Descriptions of Lexington's cultural growth are in Bernard Mayo, "Lexington: Frontier Metropolis," in *Historiography and Urbanization: Essays in American History in Honor of W. Stull Holt,* ed. Eric F. Goldman (Baltimore, 1941), pp. 31–40, and Richard C. Wade, *The Urban Frontier: The Rise of Western Cities, 1790–1830* (Cambridge, Mass., 1959), pp. 233–239.

14Quoted in Richard C. Wade, "Urban Life in Western America, 1790–1830," *American Historical Review* 64 (October, 1958): 25.

"frequent arguments and debates held in what we termed 'Rocky Mountain College.' "[15] Even such an illiterate old reprobate as Jim Bridger was never happier than when a companion was reading Shakespeare beside the campfire. On one such occasion the tale of the murder of the two princes in the Tower aroused him to a violent denunciation of the Bard, who, he declared, "must have had a bad heart and been as devilish mean as a Sioux, to have written such scoundrelism as that."[16]

Many cowboys, whose secession from civilization was almost complete, were equally avid readers, even though books were virtually nonexistent on the Plains. Some were so starved for literary fare that they read and re-read the labels on tins in the cook's shack until they could recite every one from memory, syllable by syllable. Tenderfeet who did not "know their cans" were made social outcasts when a cowboy would shout a key phrase and the whole group would chant in unison the words on every label in the ranch. When mail order catalogs appeared, they were memorized just as completely. One cattleman was so eager for unfamiliar words that he reined in his horse when he saw a scrap of paper on the ground. "I got down and picked it up," he later recalled, "simply because I was hungry for something to read, if not more than two or three words." Another read a patent medicine advertisement so often that, as

15Osborne Russell, *Journal of a Trapper; or, Nine Years in the Rocky Mountains, 1834–1843* (Boise, Idaho, 1921), pp. 55, 109.
16Frances F. Victor, *The River of the West* (Hartford, 1870), pp. 83–85. An interesting study showing that the mountain men not only longed to return to civilization but also usually did so is in William H. Goetzmann, "The Mountain Man as Jacksonian Man," *American Quarterly* 15 (Fall, 1963): 402–415.

he later wrote, he convinced himself that he had the symptoms of seven different diseases, all fatal.[17]

If the urge to read could touch such cultural outcasts as cowboys and fur trappers, it would have a far greater impact on the small-farmers who made up the bulk of the frontier population. These yeomen needed sturdier literary fare than labels or scraps of paper; books alone would do, and in such quantity and variety that the readers would not lose touch with eastern civilization. The extent of their craving was revealed both by the demands on publishers and by the multiplication of bookstores and libraries.

Publishers during the pre–Civil War era freely admitted that sales in the West made the difference between profits and bankruptcy. During the winter, when frozen rivers ended contact with the frontier, a number of publishers closed their doors entirely while others operated on a reduced scale. "The publishing season," wrote a New York author in mid-November, 1845, "is now nearly closed, [and when] the rivers are frozen . . . it will be over." James Fenimore Cooper was told by his Philadelphia publisher in 1832 that an unexpectedly early freeze had hurt the sales of his latest book. So important were western sales that the reputations of authors were made or broken beyond the Appalachians; an editor explained to Henry Wadsworth Longfellow that top royalties could not be paid to James Russell Lowell because he enjoyed no reputation in the West. "I know," he said, "the test of *general* popularity as well

[17]Don D. Walker, "Reading on the Range: The Literary Habits of the American Cowboy," *Arizona and the West* 2 (Winter, 1960): 307–318.

as any man—and he has it not. He is well known in New England and appreciated there but has not a tythe of the reputation *South and West* possessed by yourself and Bryant."[18]

Westerners' thirst for reading matter spelled opportunity to booksellers. One had this forcefully brought home when, in 1804, he crossed upper New York State to start a shop in Toronto. At Canandaigua, then a primitive hamlet on a raw frontier, he was physically captured and held until he agreed to open a bookstore there.[19] The story was the same everywhere; travelers never ceased to marvel that pioneer villages could support booksellers in surprising numbers. Lexington, Kentucky, contained less than seven hundred inhabitants in 1788, yet six dealers advertised books for sale. Eight years later Cincinnati's five hundred settlers could choose between two bookstores, one of which advertised "books of divinity, law and physic, several entertaining histories; some English and Latin school books; a variety of books for the instruction and entertainment of children; American magazines and museums of the latest date."[20] Davenport, Iowa, boasted its first bookstore

18An excellent discussion of this subject is in William Charvat, *Literary Publishing in America, 1790–1850* (Philadelphia, 1959), pp. 18–25.

19This story is told in a brief biography of this bookseller, James D. Bemis, in Madeleine B. Stern, *Imprints on History: Book Publishers and American Frontiers* (Bloomington, Ind., 1956), pp. 5–23.

20Howard H. Peckham, "Books and Readings on the Ohio Valley Frontier," *Mississippi Valley Historical Review* 44 (March, 1958): 652–653. For additional information see Wade, *The Urban Frontier*, p. 140, and Wright, *Culture on the Moving Frontier*, pp. 71–75. Comparable information on frontier Pittsburgh is in Edward P. Anderson, "Intellectual Life of Pittsburgh, 1786–1836," *Western Pennsylvania Historical Magazine* 14 (April, 1931): 103–105.

when the town was less than three years old and the population under five hundred.[21] Even the boisterous mining camps of the Forty-Niners supported an itinerant peddler who advertised "the works of Shakespeare, Byron, Milton, Gray, Campbell and other distinguished poets."[22] Clearly the frontiersmen could shame modern Americans, for few villages of today provide such cultural opportunities.

Libraries also mushroomed on successive frontiers, providing as they did reading matter for literature-starved pioneers by distributing the cost among many. Dayton, Ohio, founded its first subscription library in 1805 when the town was less than ten years old and the population below one hundred; so eager were the first subscribers that they drew lots to decide who were to see the volumes when the shipment arrived. Cleveland's first library was established in 1811 when sixteen of the sixty-four inhabitants pooled their resources to buy books. In Madison, Indiana, all twenty-four male inhabitants of the village contributed five dollars each to finance the initial book purchases.[23] Of the group of pioneer farmers near Belpré, Ohio, who pledged ten

[21]Joseph S. Schick, *The Early Theater in Eastern Iowa* (Chicago, 1939), pp. 161–165. Despite its title, this is a competent study of all intellectual activity.

[22]Stern, *Imprints on History*, pp. 137–138.

[23]The history of subscription libraries in the Mississippi Valley is told in such works as Eleonora A. Baer, "Books, Newspapers, and Libraries in Pioneer St. Louis, 1808–1842," *Missouri Historical Review* 56 (July, 1962): 358–360; W. T. Norton, "Early Libraries in Illinois," *Journal of the Illinois State Historical Society* 6 (July, 1913): 246–251; William H. Venable, *Beginnings of Literary Culture in the Ohio Valley* (Cincinnati, 1891), pp. 263–264; and Wade, *The Urban Frontier*, pp. 254–256. A detailed case study of one such library is J. F. Waring, *Books and Reading in Hudson, 1800–1954: A History of the Hudson Library and Historical Society* (Hudson, Ohio, 1954).

dollars each in 1796 to launch the first library in that territory, one later recalled his thrill when the volumes were delivered. "I had," he wrote, "no candles; however the woods afforded plenty of pine knots—and with these I made torches by which I could read, though I nearly spoiled my eyes. Many a night I have passed in this manner till 12 or 1 o'clock reading to my wife, while she was hatchelling, carding or spinning."[24]

Most famous among these pioneer institutions was the "Coonskin Library" of Ohio. It began in 1803 when the farmers of Ames Township gathered to plan a library similar to that in Belpré. Plagued by the usual shortage of cash, they agreed to donate the proceeds of a winter's trapping and hunting to a Western Library Association, founded on the spot to provide "the many beneficial effects which social libraries are calculated to produce in societies." With furs gathered by twenty-four persons, Samuel Brown took off for Boston that spring, there to sell the pelts for seventy dollars. He returned with fifty-one volumes, including Goldsmith's works, Ramsay's *History of the American Revolution*, Playfair's *History of Jacobinism*, Harris's *Minor Encyclopedia*, Morse's *Geography*, and a sampling of biography and history. When these treasures were dumped from saddlebags to a cabin floor, the awestruck members felt, as one of them wrote, that "the library of the Vatican seemed a mere trifle by comparison."[25]

Frontiersmen obviously wanted books, but the ques-

24Henry Howe, *Historical Collections of Ohio* (Cincinnati, 1847), p. 349.
25Sarah J. Cutler, "The Coonskin Library," *Ohio Archaeological and Historical Quarterly* 26 (January, 1917): 58–77.

tion remains: did they demand practical books about the West that would mirror their own lives or ease the hardships of pioneering? Or were they content to savor the traditional literary fare that revealed their unwillingness to break with their cultural heritage? Such data as are available on the reading tastes of the pioneers suggest that they demanded books then popular in Europe and the East or that they had known in their childhoods rather than western novels or essays. Of the 2,000 titles purchased by five libraries on the Ohio Valley frontier before 1815, about 30 percent were literary classics, 15 percent legal and political studies, 13 percent well-known histories, and the remainder traditional books on religion, science, and travel. Scott, Shakespeare, Goldsmith, and Pope were the most popular authors, although Byron was in great demand and such American writers as Joel Barlow had some following.[26] Western publishers catered to somewhat different interests; of the 567 books printed in the Ohio Valley during the pioneer period, 29 percent were almanacs and gazetteers, 23 percent religious works, 17 percent instructional books, and only 12 percent novels or essays. Local publishing houses, aware of the practical needs of the frontiersmen, apparently sensed the need for self-help and religious books that would ease the lot of the pioneers in this world and the next.[27]

Significantly, publishers in both East and West

[26]James M. Miller, *The Genesis of Western Culture: The Upper Ohio Valley, 1800–1825* (Columbus, 1938), pp. 147–151; Ralph L. Rusk, *The Literature of the Middle Western Frontier* (New York, 1925), II, 1–38.

[27]Peckham, "Books and Reading on the Ohio Valley Frontier," pp. 657–660, thoroughly analyzes western publishing trends.

failed to detect any major interest in books about frontier life. Scott and Goldsmith were far more popular among the pioneers than Washington Irving or James Fenimore Cooper, perhaps because westerners were repelled by the distorted pictures of frontiersmen presented by those authors. Nor were books by western writers any more popular, for they closed their eyes to the pulsating frontier about them and wrote instead of eastern scenes and eastern events. They, like their readers, were too eager to maintain cultural ties with the East to recognize the lusty young civilization they were helping to create. One western writer who inflicted on the world a life of George Washington written in Latin, and another who penned a four-volume effusion called *Fredoniad; or, Independence Preserved, an Epic Poem on the Late War of 1812*, testify to the dreadful results of the cult of eastern worship that persisted among the pioneers.[28]

They testify also to the eagerness of frontiersmen to perpetuate in the West the familiar cultural patterns of the East. This was to be expected. Reading is more than a pleasure; it is a habit to which one can become forever addicted. Migrants who had succumbed would normally take with them or import only the most prized literary treasures, for transportation was expensive; these classics were read and re-read in their new homes with an interest that would have been impossible in the

28Logan Esarey, "The Literary Spirit Among the Early Ohio Valley Settlers," *Mississippi Valley Historical Review* 5 (September, 1918): 148–153, gives many examples of this type of writing. Others are in R. Carlyle Buley, *The Old Northwest: Pioneer Period, 1815–1840* (Indianapolis, 1950), II, 558–562, and Rusk, *The Literature of the Middle Western Frontier*, II, 272–351.

East, where the complexity of society created many diversions. Pioneers with such appetites became masters of a limited body of reading matter that was valued for its scarcity no less than for its intrinsic worth. They were, as a result, more closely bound to a traditional culture than were easterners, who had a wider fare from which to pick and choose. An Ohio Valley frontiersman mirrored this veneration of traditionalism when he wrote in 1820: "Should the time ever come when Latin and Greek should be banished from our universities, and the study of Cicero and Demosthenes, or Homer and Virgil should be considered as unnecessary for the formation of a scholar, we should regard mankind as fast sinking into absolute barbarism, and the gloom of mental darkness as likely to increase until it should become universal."[29]

Yet strive as they did to re-create in their new homes the civilization of the old, they were destined to failure. All unbeknownst to the pioneers, environmental forces were reshaping their cultural interests no less than their living patterns. The result was not barbarism, but a new culture based on tradition but significantly altered. This transformation was predestined by the nature of the migration process and by the demands of frontiering.

Frontiers naturally attracted men of action and material ambition rather than the studious and the contemplative. In the sifting that occurred as the westward movement went on, those with the greatest intel-

[29]*Western Review* 3 (1820): 145. For the persistence of classical interests, see Walter A. Agard, "Classics on the Midwest Frontier," in *The Frontier in Perspective*, ed. Walker D. Wyman and Clifton B. Kroeber (Madison, Wis., 1957), pp. 165–183.

lectual interests were left behind; even the "better sort" who reached the West determined to plant culture there soon found themselves so absorbed in mercantile activity that there was too little time left for learning. Those who retained their enthusiasm for study were handicapped by the atomization of society along the frontiers; cultural progress is always greatest where men of like interests live elbow to elbow and can benefit from cooperation and mutual encouragement. In the West such men were so isolated that contact was difficult. These conditions dampened the ability of the few cultured pioneers to improve upon and popularize their learning.

A still more serious handicap was the materialistic atmosphere normal in new regions. In a land where material tasks absorbed the population's energy, so many practical needs existed that those who frittered away their time in cultural pursuits seemed to be neglecting their duty to society. The writer, the artist, or even the reader was squandering time that might better be spent providing food and shelter. The frontiersman, observed an acute French traveler, "is obliged to occupy himself much more with the cultivation of the earth, than of himself."[30] When a New Englander sought to elevate the tone of the frontier Indiana school that had hired him as a teacher, he was told by one youth: "Daddy says he doesn't see no sort of use in the high larn'd things—and he wants me to larn Inglish only, and book keepin, and surveyin, so as to tend store and run a line."[31]

[30]Michael Chevalier, *Society, Manners and Politics in the United States* (Boston, 1839), p. 220.

[31]Hall, *The New Purchase*, II, 83. Similar comments by pioneers are in Harriet Brown, *Grandmother Brown's Hundred Years, 1827-1927*

[68]

This necessary stress on practical ends created an atmosphere hostile to the perpetuation of traditional cultural pursuits. Utility became the test of any activity, and woe unto the pioneer who deviated from this behavioral pattern. The folk heroes of the West were men of accomplishment rather than contemplation; Davy Crockett and Daniel Boone were venerated, not Dr. Daniel Drake or Timothy Flint. Andrew Jackson was the idol of the frontiersmen not because he was a capable businessman or a successful diplomat, but because he was an Indian fighter and a champion of the "true-grit West" against the effete East. Said an observer who knew the pioneers well: "A wheat field is more pleasing to their taste than a flower garden. A well-ploughed lot is more satisfactory to their eye than the most exquisite painting of a Raphael or a Claude. They would prefer seeing a gristmill working on their own stream, to the sight of the sculptured marble of the Venus or the Apollo."[32] These same prejudices were voiced with less elegance by a pioneer Michigan housewife, who, when she saw a neighbor planting flowers, sniffed that "she'd never know'd nobody make nothin' by raisin' sich things."[33]

These attitudes spelled failure for those who sought to perpetuate the East's culture among westerners The cultivated "better sort" might found circulating libraries and enliven their conversation with quotations from Homer, but they fought a losing battle. Historians eager

(Boston, 1929), p. 133, and Eliza W. Farnham, *Life in Prairie Land* (New York, 1846), pp. 330–331.

32James H. Lanman, "The Progress of the Northwest," *Hunt's Merchants' Magazine* 3 (July–December 1840): 39.

33Caroline M. Kirkland, *A New Home—Who'll Follow? or, Glimpses of Western Life* (New York, 1839), p. 135.

to prove the transit of culture westward have made much of the fact that by 1812 Kentucky had eleven subscription libraries, Ohio ten, and Indiana two. Yet this was only one library for every 37,000 persons in Kentucky, one for every 23,760 in Ohio, and one for every 12,260 in Indiana. The great mass of the people had no access to books, and probably couldn't have cared less. Men of lofty ambition might establish fine magazines such as Timothy Flint's *Western Monthly Review* or James Hall's *Western Monthly Magazine*, but not one of those publications survived public apathy for more than a few years. Perhaps Ralph Waldo Emerson exaggerated when he wrote disgustedly after a lecture tour in the West that the people "in all that is called cultivation [were] only ten years old," but he came uncomfortably near to the truth.[34] Rebellion against culture became the hallmark of many a pioneer amidst the materialistic atmosphere of his adopted world. One Tennessee town promoter, seeking to attract settlers by assuring those about him that they would achieve "civilization, intelligence, comfort, and health" if they worked hard, was told in no uncertain terms that they had come westward to escape civilization, and that if it followed them they would move on.[35] The members of the Sacramento literary society who devoted meetings to spinning a hat to see who would pay for drinks may not have typified frontier culture, but they came dangerously close to doing so.[36]

[34]Ralph Waldo Emerson, *The Journals of Ralph Waldo Emerson* (Boston, 1909–1914), IX, 4.

[35]Quoted in F. Garvin Davenport, "Culture versus Frontier in Tennessee, 1825–1850," *Journal of Southern History* 5 (February, 1939): 24.

[36]Frank Marryat, *Mountains and Molehills; or, Recollections of a Burnt Journal* (London, 1855), p. 224.

Clearly the frontier was not an area of transplanted eastern culture, complete with eastern values and institutions, any more than it was a region where barbarians triumphed over civilization. Nor could the successive Wests be correctly characterized as zones in transition between the savagery of the forest and the matured civilizations of Europe and the East. Instead, the frontier was a land where imported cultural patterns were modified to conform to the unique conditions that existed where untapped natural resources afforded unusual opportunity to incoming settlers. This adjustment, prompted primarily by the materialistic attitude bred into the pioneers by the demands of frontiering, contributed to two enduring changes in American civilization.

One was the emergence of a spirit of anti-intellectualism that has haunted cultural progress down to the present. The frontier heritage was not the only force that created a people who enshrined the practical man as their god, but the stress on utilitarianism in newer communities was a major influence. Wrote a disgusted clergyman from the early backcountry: "Instead of honouring a Learned Person, or any one of Wit and Knowledge . . . they despise and ill treat them."[37] This attitude has persisted; even today the intellectual who would be venerated in nonfrontier European nations is ridiculed as an "egghead" who has little to contribute in a land where the business of the people is business.[38]

[37]Quoted in Carl Bridenbaugh, *Myths and Realities: Societies of the Colonial South* (Baton Rouge, 1952), p. 191.

[38]Merle Curti, "Intellectuals and Other People," *American Historical Review* 60 (January, 1955): 259–282, deals expertly with the frontier influence on American anti-intellectualism, a subject less well

Another, and happier, result of the frontiering experience was a rebellion against romanticism in the arts and the substitution of a creative realism that has recast literature, painting, education, and all cultural expression in a new mold. Again, pioneering was not solely responsible—all the western world forsook romanticism for realism in the nineteenth and early twentieth centuries—but the banner of rebellion was raised first in western communities. There, romanticism seemed not only outmoded but outlandish; gushing effusions of poets extolling the beauties of nature would have little appeal to frontiersmen who saw trees as enemies that must be destroyed. "We confess," wrote a westerner in the 1830's, "we are heartily tired of the endless imitations of Scott, Byron, and Moore, and the rest of them, and stand ready to welcome something new, even though it should smack a little of the 'Horse,' contain a touch of the 'Alligator,' and betray a small sprinkling of the 'Steamboat.' "[39]

In the world of letters, that "something new" took the form of a lusty realism rooted in the southwestern frontier. Augustus Baldwin Longstreet, with his *Georgia Scenes* of cockfights, horse swappings, and gander pullings; Johnson J. Hooper, whose hawk-nosed hero, Simon Suggs, admirably lived up to his motto, "It's good to be shifty in a new country"; and Joseph G. Baldwin, with his *Flush Times in Alabama and Mississippi*, were her-

comprehended in Richard Hofstadter, *Anti-Intellectualism in American Life* (New York, 1963). A savage indictment of the frontier as a breeder of anti-intellectualism is in Arthur K. Moore, *The Frontier Mind: A Cultural Analysis of the Kentucky Frontiersman* (Lexington, Ky, 1957).
[39]Quoted in Buley, *The Old Northwest*, II, 563.

alds of realistic literature because they found in the West scenes and characters that defied traditional description. "It would indeed seem," wrote one of their contemporaries, "that the nearer sundown, the more original the character and odd the expression."[40] When this literary form flowered a generation later in the works of Bret Harte and Mark Twain, American writing had won its independence from the European heritage.[41]

These stirrings in the literary world exemplify the impact of the frontier on America's cultural growth. The pioneers did not want change; the effort of the "better sort" and the common folk alike was to replant in the West the civilization of the East. They failed, for the social environment of the new communities, with its emphasis on the practical, provided sterile soil for the flowering of traditional cultural forms. Instead, the realistic value scale of the frontiersmen fostered new social attitudes and new literary forms that were better tuned to the world in which they lived. These innovations were the West's unique contribution to the nation's burgeoning culture.

[40]John S. Robb, *Streaks of Squatter Life and Far West Scenes* (Philadelphia, 1847), p. viii.
[41]Since the 1920's one school of literary historians has assigned the frontier a major role in reshaping the character of American writing. For statements of their case, see Jay B. Hubbell, "The Frontier in American Literature," *Southwest Review* 10 (January, 1925): 84–92; Percy H. Boynton, *The Rediscovery of the Frontier* (Chicago, 1931); and Arlin Turner, "Seeds of Literary Revolt in the Humor of the Old Southwest," *Louisiana Historical Quarterly* 39 (April, 1956): 143–151.

# Cowboys, Indians, and the Land of Promise

I am sure most people will agree when I say that the "Wild, Wild West" is alive and well in much of the world today, nearly a century after the last cowboy blazed a path of virtue across the Great Plains with his six-shooters and the last Apache unleashed his arrows against the encircled wagon train. The myth of the American frontier as a land of romance, violence, and personal justice has persisted and grown, to influence popular attitudes toward the United States and its policies down to the present.

The persuasive influence of the frontier image is nowhere better exhibited than by the cultists of other nations who try to recapture life in that never-never land of the past. In Paris, western addicts buy outfits at a store near the Arc de Triomphe called the Western

Delivered as the opening plenary address before the Fourteenth International Congress of the Historical Sciences on August 22, 1975, under the title "Cowboys, Indians, and the Land of Promise: The World Image of the American Frontier," and subsequently published in *Proceedings of the XIV International Congress of the Historical Sciences* (New York, 1976), pp. 60–79.

[74]

House, spend weekends at Camp Indien clad in Comanche headdresses and moccasins, or don cowboy sombreros and spurred boots to gallop through the Bois de Boulogne—on Vespas. Frontier buffs have brought affluence to the late George Fronval, a novelist who has written nearly six hundred "westerns," fifty-four of them about Buffalo Bill Cody, under such improbable titles as *The Cavern of the Mammoths* and *The Prisoner of the Ku Klux Klan*.[1]

In Austria children play "cowboys and Indians" or walk "Indian file" through the cobbled streets, their makeshift costumes contrasting strangely with half-timbered houses. In West Germany enthusiasts buy Rodeo Aftershave and a deodorant called Lasso, purchase western clothes from two thriving chain stores (some buffs refuse to watch westerns on television unless properly garbed), and belong to one of the sixty-three societies in the Western Clubs Federation whose members spend weekends in log houses, dress as Sioux Indians or cowboys, and carry realism to the uncomfortable extreme of using saddles for pillows and barring Indian impersonators from the club saloon.[2] In Norway a "western" hero, Morgan Kane, is a national favorite

[1]Charles J. Belden, "The Spirit of the Old West Still Lives in Paris," *Horse Lover's Magazine* 27 (December, 1961–January, 1962): 30–31; Jeffrey Robinson, "Le Cowboy," *Westways* 66 (April, 1974): 40–41; Kent L. Steckmesser, "Paris and the Wild West," *Southwest Review* 54 (Spring, 1969): 172–173.

[2]Thomas Freeman, "The Cowboy and the Astronaut—The American Image in German Periodical Advertisements," *Journal of Popular Culture* 6 (Summer, 1972): 90–91; D. L. Ashliman, "The American West in Twentieth-Century Germany," *Journal of Popular Culture* 2 (Summer, 1968): 82–92; "Western Stores," *Der Spiegel* 18 (April 15, 1964): 64; "Europe's Fascination with Old West Shows in Clubs," *Los Angeles Times*, December 9, 1973.

[75]

among the young; in Japan, Frontier restaurants vie for customers, and a *Frontier* magazine has recently appeared.[3]

So irresistible is the compulsion to imitate western heroes that a Glasgow health officer not long ago lamented that Scottish lads were becoming round-shouldered and hollow-chested from copying the slouching stride of cowboys.[4] Blue jeans transcend international boundaries in their appeal even though, as in the Soviet Union, they cost a full month's pay—and authentic Levi's even more.[5] Nor do elders set a different example; when Soviet party leader Leonid I. Brezhnev visited President Nixon in 1973, the one person he greeted with bear-hug enthusiasm was Chuck Connors, the hero of a television series called "The Rifleman."[6]

All these people are responding to the image of the American West projected by twentieth-century films, novels, and television programs: a sun-drenched land of distant horizons peopled largely by scowling bad men in black shirts, villainous Indians, and those Galahads of the Plains, the cowboys, glamorous in hip-hugging Levi's and embroidered shirts, a pair of Colt revolvers worn low about the hips. A land, too, of the shoot-out, individual justice, and sudden death at the hands of

[3]Masaharu Watanabe, "The Japanese Images of the American West since 1868," unpublished manuscript; Ingrid Semmingsen to author, September 8, 1973.

[4]*Denver Post*, September 19, 1963, quoted in Clifford P. Westermeier, "Clio's Maverick–the Cowboy," *Denver Westerner's Monthly Roundup* 22 (October, 1966): 13.

[5]"U.S. Jeans: The Hottest Thing Going in Russia," *Los Angeles Times*, November 20, 1973; N. N. Bolkhovitinov to author, January 23, 1975.

[6]*Los Angeles Times*, November 29, 1973.

lynch mobs. Recently an Israeli army psychologist, pleased that his country's soldiers did not use their weapons while on leave, expressed delight that "There is no shooting like in the Wild West."[7]

It is easy to understand that such an image should be popular today. To empathize with a make-believe land of masculinity and self-realization is to forget momentarily the monotony of a routinized, mechanized civilization, to escape the uncertainties of a turbulent world, and to recapture an unregimented past. The vogue of a "western" cult demonstrates a universal urge to lessen the controls necessary in today's societies.

To understand that vogue is relatively easy; to trace the genesis of the frontier image demands a more extended analysis. Images do not emerge overnight, nor are they unrelated to the experiences of their holders. Instead, they customarily define the past in terms of today's values and evolve in directions governed by the psychological needs of the present. How, then, has the frontier image now current been shaped by prior experiences and modified to meet modern emotional needs?

The modern concept of the American West blends two different images that emerged during the eighteenth and nineteenth centuries. One pictured the frontier as lawless, brutal, and repelling, molded by a savage environment that reduced the frontiersmen to semibarbarism. The other painted the West as a transplanted Eden, overflowing with the bounties of nature and beckoning the dispossessed to a new life of abundance

[7]Ibid., February 19, 1975.

and freedom. How did these conflicting images emerge and persist during the nineteenth century?

The myth of the frontier as a land of violence and lawlessness was the invention primarily of imaginative novelists and prejudiced travelers. The travelers who visited the West during the late eighteenth and nineteenth centuries can be counted by the hundreds; more than fifty of their accounts were published in Germany in the thirty years after 1815, more than two hundred in England, nearly forty in Japan after 1868, dozens in France and Italy, and eight in Hungary.[8] The picture they painted was shaped by political bias; conservatives exaggerated the brutalizing impact of frontier democracy on men and institutions, while liberals overstressed the virtues of manhood suffrage and social equality. Both conservative and liberal, however, were shocked by the crudities of western life and the contrast between the cultural sophistication of their homelands and the primitive societies they encountered on the borderlands.

Even more influential than travelers as image makers were novelists. James Fenimore Cooper set the example; his *Leatherstocking Tales* about the New York frontier took Europe by storm. They were translated into a dozen languages, sold hundreds of thousands of copies, and continue to be read today; in Russia alone, thirty-four editions of Cooper's collected works have been published, two of them since 1917.[9] Such popu-

[8]Jane L. Mesick, *The English Traveler in America, 1785–1835* (New York, 1922); Max Berger, *The British Traveller in America, 1836–1860* (New York, 1943); John C. Brooks, *As Others See Us* (New York, 1953); Anna Katona, "Hungarian Travelogues on the Pre–Civil War U.S.," *Hungarian Studies in English* 5 (1971): 51–56.

[9]Robert Magidoff, "American Literature in Russia," *Saturday*

larity inspired imitation, and in Cooper's wake a host of novelists turned to the American West as a scene for their adventures:

In England, Mayne Reid and Percy St. John; in France, Gustave Aimard and Gabriel Ferry; in Italy, Emilio Salgari; in Germany, Charles Sealsfield, Friedrich Gerstäcker, and Balduin Möllhausen. (To single out these few is to do an injustice to dozens more.) All were prolific writers (Balduin Möllhausen wrote more than 150 books, and most of the others as many as 30), and all were translated widely.[10] Their school of literature (if it may be thus called) was climaxed at the end of the century when Karl May introduced the ultimate *Westmann*, Old Shatterhand, and his faithful Indian companion, Winnetou, to the German public. May's 70 novels have sold thirty million copies in more than twenty languages, and they still sell about one million copies yearly. An annual Karl May Festival in West Germany attracts some 150,000 of the dedicated; Karl May films, Karl May plays, and Karl May toys have

---

*Review of Literature* 29 (November 2, 1946): 9. On Cooper's influence, see Willard Thorp, "Cooper Beyond America," *New York History* 35 (October, 1854): 522–539, and Preston A. Barba, "Cooper in Germany," *Indiana University Studies*, no. 21 (1914): 52–104.

10Particularly useful is D. L. Ashliman, "The American West in Nineteenth-Century German Literature," Ph.D. diss., Rutgers University, 1969 (Ann Arbor: University Microfilms, 1969). He summarizes some of his findings in "The Novel of Western Adventure in Nineteenth-Century Germany," *Western American Literature* 3 (Summer, 1968): 133–145. An earlier and more general study is Paul C. Weber, *America in Imaginative German Literature in the First Half of the Nineteenth Century* (New York, 1926). Briefer are Carl Wittke, "The American Theme in Continental European Literature," *Mississippi Valley Historical Review* 28 (June, 1941): 3–26, and George B. Brooks, "The American Frontier in German Fiction," in *The Frontier Re-examined*, ed. John F. McDermott (Urbana, Ill., 1967), pp. 155–167.

captivated, and still captivate, a sizable portion of Europe's population.[11]

The American West pictured by these sensation peddlers was an unbelievable fantasy land where savage animals and equally savage Indians lurked in tropical forests, where fights with daggers and revolvers were part of the daily routine, and where life was of uncertain duration for all not prepared to kill an opponent before he could whip his bowie knife from its sheath or his .45 from its holster. Certainly this Wild West bore not the faintest resemblance to the West that was: a West of sweating farmers, cowboys who more often worked in derby hats than sombreros (and many of whom were Negroes or Mexican Americans), and law-abiding citizens whose principal objective was to reproduce the orderly societies of the East as rapidly as possible. Why this distortion?

Ignorance was not always the answer. Karl May did not visit the United States until just before his death, but other novelists knew the frontier well; Charles Sealsfield lived for years in the Southwest, much of Gustave Aimard's youth was spent beyond the Mississippi, and Balduin Möllhausen gained his first fame while accompanying exploring expeditions into the Rocky Mountain

[11]Richard H. Cracroft, "The American West of Karl May," M.A. thesis, University of Utah, 1963, is the best treatment in English. The author summarizes his findings in "The American West of Karl May," *American Quarterly* 19 (Summer, 1967): 249–258. Also useful are Ernst A. Stadler, "Karl May: The Wild West under the German Umlaut," *Missouri Historical Society Bulletin* 21 (July, 1965): 295–307; Ralph W. Walker, "The Wonderful West of Karl May," *American West* 10 (November, 1973): 28–33; and "Karl der Deutsche," *Der Spiegel* 16 (September 12, 1962): 54–74. May's current popularity is described in "Germans Playing at Cowboys, Indians," *Los Angeles Times*, June 17, 1973.

country. Yet truth cramped their writing but slightly. Instead, their imaginative creations were molded to the tastes of their sensation-seeking audiences, who then, as now, thirsted for vicarious thrills. A Texan visiting in London during the 1840's realized this desire for excitement when he met some of England's most eminent intellectuals. "They listened with deference to all that I said," he reported, "but . . . with delight to the accounts of our Indian fights, Prairie life, and buffalo hunts."[12] The temptation to cater to the whims of readers who demanded ever more excitement was too profitable to be resisted.

Some of the exaggerations of novelists and travelers can be forgiven as typical—and delightful—tall tales. No reader could possibly believe that the soil in Arkansas was so rich that settlers made candles by dipping wicks in mud puddles or that land in Kansas was so fertile that it produced fifty bushels of maize to the acre when none had been planted.[13] Nor could the most gullible take seriously the account of a buffalo hunt in which an Indian was caught in the middle of a stampeding herd but escaped by leaping from back to back of the charging beasts, pausing in his flight to lance some of the fattest cows.[14]

But less excusable were fantasies only slightly less unbelievable: the Gila River Valley (actually an arid desert) teeming with alligators, monstrous boa constric-

[12]G. W. Terrell to W. D. Miller, January 20, 1845, quoted in Mark E. Nackman, *A Nation Within a Nation: The Rise of Texas Nationalism* (Port Washington, N.Y., 1975), p. 8.

[13]Friedrich Gerstäcker, *Alapaha, the Squaw; or, The Renegades of the Border* (London, 1850), pp. 63–64.

[14]Robert M. Ballantyne, *The Dog Crusoe: A Tale of the Western Prairies* (London, 1861), pp. 94–95.

tors, and giant basilisks "crawling silent and sinister beneath the leaves"; an Apache heroine, "White Gazelle," dressed in "loose Turkish trowsers, made of Indian cashmere, fastened at the knees with diamond garters . . . while a jacket of violet velvet, buttoned over the bosom with a profusion of diamonds, displayed her exquisite bust"; an earthquake that sloshed the Colorado River over its banks to quench a forest fire that threatened the hero; an ostrich hunt staged by the Blackfoot Indians of Montana that ended with a great feast, "for the ostrich is excellent eating, and the Indians prepare, chiefly from the meat on the breast, a dish renowned for its delicacy and exquisite flavor."[15]

Novelists and travelers paid only slightly more tribute to actuality when they described the frontiersmen who peopled these wilds. Three types were identified: "Hunters," who roamed far ahead of the settlements; "Squatters," who made the first assault on the wilderness; and "Pioneers," who extended their clearings and heralded the first coming of civilization. Actually, there was little to distinguish these stereotypes; all three represented stages in the degradation of civilized man. Yet the image makers elevated the Hunter, who was actually the least savory of the lot, to the role of hero, picturing him as a godlike superman ennobled spiritually by daily contact with nature.

The Hunter was a type long familiar to readers and hence demanded by them—a reincarnation of the "child of nature" so glorified in eighteenth-century romanti-

[15]Gustave Aimard, *The Pirates of the Prairies: Adventures in the American Desert* (London, 1862), pp. 20, 50–51, 146–152; Gustave Aimard, *The Prairie-Flower: A Tale of the Indian Border* (London, 186?), pp. 24–25.

cism. Reared in the forests' haunting silence, these "primitive-strong" (as a German writer named them) blended the best of primitivism and civilization.[16] Cruel they were, for they must kill the Indians who blocked their countrymen's path westward, but their cruelty was transcended by an inner nobility, a God-given nobility, the gift of intimacy with the Creator through His creations. "Among them," wrote a German novelist, "I have observed a genius which would have done honor to the greatest philosophers of ancient and modern times."[17] He was speaking, mind you, of semibarbarians, most of them illiterate, who had traded civilization's restraints for savagery's brutal freedom.

The Squatters, by contrast, were depicted as near animals who had rejected civilization without acquiring any of nature's blessings. "The very outcasts of society," they were called, "the scum and the dregs."[18] Sunk in sloth and laziness, they were destined to flee forever from normal humans. The Pioneers were little better. They were pictured as crude, boastful, ill-mannered braggarts, living slovenly lives and disdainful of the higher values that distinguished civilized men from barbarians.

Image makers delighted in isolating traits of the Pioneers that they found especially annoying. One of those traits was eternal boasting. Travelers reported

16Augustus J. Prahl, "America in the Works of Gerstäcker," *Modern Language Quarterly* 4 (June, 1943): 224.

17Charles Sealsfield, *The Courtship of George Howard* (London, 1843), p. 43.

18Ibid., pp. 212–214; Hugo Munsterberg, *American Traits from the Point of View of a German* (New York, 1902), p. 9; Matilda J. F. Houstoun, *Hesperos; or, Travels in the West* (London, 1850), II, 49.

listening to an incessant litany of self-praise: "The Americans were *more* learned, *more* powerful, and altogether *more* extraordinary than any other people in the world."[19] The United States, its citizens bragged, had the most fertile soils, the strongest armies, the biggest cities, the largest rivers, the noisiest thunder, and (according to one traveler) the longest history of any nation on the globe. Conversely, the rest of the world was a decaying ruin. Asia was a heathen backwash doomed to perpetual misrule; Europe was sunk in despotism and poverty—"A heap of medieval feudal states . . . that have not enough vitality to rise from the abyss of misery and corruption into which they have fallen as a result of centuries of ignorance and despotism."[20] The New World was outstripping the Old; soon England would be known only as the mother of the United States.[21]

Just as annoying as the constant "puffing" (to use the language of the day) were the abominable manners of the Squatters and Pioneers. Their principal offense against good taste was their constant tobacco chewing. Along the frontiers, said the image makers, all men's jaws were perpetually in motion as they chewed and spit, chewed and spit, for all the world (to quote a Polish observer) "as though they were some species of ruminating animal."[22] The entire West, indoors and

[19]Houstoun, *Hesperos*, II, 25.

[20]Ole Munch Raeder, *America in the Forties: The Letters of Ole Munch Raeder* (Minneapolis, 1929), p. 83.

[21]Frederick Marryat, *A Diary in America* (London, 1839), II, 89.

[22]Henryk Sienkiewicz, *Portrait of America: Letters of Henry Sienkiewicz* (New York, 1959), p. 20. The letters were originally published in Polish magazines and newspapers between 1876 and 1878.

out, was carpeted with dried tobacco juice, while spitters were a constant menace even though most were good shots; "when you are surrounded with shooters," one traveler wrote feelingly, "you feel nervous."[23] So universal was the habit that the twang noticeable in western speech was ascribed to the fact that westerners' mouths were always so full of juice that they could not be opened without overflowing, forcing the Pioneers to speak through their noses.[24]

Above all, the frontier was a Babylon of barbarism. On the Mississippi Valley frontier, rough-and-tumble fights occurred daily, with each battler striving to bite off the nose, claw off the ears, or gouge out the eyes of his opponent. Eye gouging particularly lent itself to gory descriptions; travelers devoted page after page to imaginary battles that ended with one fighter plunging his thumbs into an enemy's eye or rising from the fray with the symbol of victory—his opponent's eyeball—held in his hand.[25] West of the Mississippi lethal battles with bowie knives and six-shooters became the stock-in-trade of the image makers, for in that Wild West of their creation every man was armed and the code of honor demanded instant retaliation for every insult, real or imagined. An English visitor, inquiring whether a revolver was necessary, was told: "Well, you mout not need one for a month, and you mout not need one for three months, but ef you ever did want one, you kin bet

[23]Edward Money, *The Truth about America* (London, 1886), p. 129.

[24]Houstoun, *Hesperos*, II, 210–211.

[25]Thomas Ashe, *Travels in America* (London, 1808), I, 225–231, contains a particularly lurid description of a gouging.

you'll want it mighty sudden."[26] Legal justice was totally lacking in this make-believe land.

The image projected by novelists and travelers—of crude, ill-mannered frontiersmen and a lawless society— was a forbidding one, and hence hardly pleasing to another group of image makers, the promoters whose purpose was to attract immigrants to the West: guidebook authors, agents for land-grant railroads eager to sell their excess holdings, propagandists for land and immigration companies, and particularly successful immigrants hoping to lure their former countrymen to the land they found so rewarding. The immigrant letters home—the "America letters," as they are called—were particularly effective, for they were believed to be utterly trustworthy. America letters spanned the oceans by the thousands during the nineteenth century; they were read in village churches and published in local newspapers, and they played a major role in picturing frontier life to the rest of the world.

The image that they projected differed so markedly from that of novelists and travelers that those who read them were forced to make a difficult decision. Should they believe that the frontier was a brutalizing wasteland, or a new Canaan assuring prosperity and freedom to all? Faced with this dilemma, some simply rejected what they disliked hearing; others accepted both images as valid, but ranked one above the other on their own value scale. A Norwegian folk ballad pictured a would-be emigrant as he pondered this decision: "I know the venture will cost me dear in the hardships of exposure

26William A. Baillie-Groham, *Camps in the Rockies* (New York, 1882), pp. 25–26.

to sun and storm, in fierce battles with scorpions and serpents and wild beasts, in deadly duels with drawn daggers. But that is better than to fight one's own people and get nothing for it."[27] That millions of Europeans and Asians decided to migrate testified to the effectiveness of the image makers who sang of the American West as a land of promise.

And what a promising land they pictured. A farm of one's own—an impossibility in most of the world—was assured to all. A penniless immigrant could hire out as a farm worker at a dollar a day, for there was work for all in the labor-hungry West. He could live on two dollars a week, saving enough each fortnight to purchase ten acres of land so fertile that it had only to be scratched to produce abundant crops.[28] With a farm of his own he was assured perpetual freedom from want or care. On the frontier all ate meat three times a day, and wood was so plentiful that cabins were never cold. More food was thrown to the dogs in a week in a frontier home than a European peasant consumed in a year. Imagine the longings of a German who seldom tasted meat while reading of a frontiersman in a western inn filling his plate twice with beef, pork, venison, chicken, turkey, and fish, then ordering a large bowl of soup because "soup trickles down . . . where beef and ham try in vain to enter."[29] He might agree with an Irish slogan:

[27]Theodore C. Blegan, ed., *Norwegian Emigrant Songs and Ballads* (Minneapolis, 1936), p. 274.

[28]*Advice to Emigrants Who Intend to Settle in the United States of America*, 2d ed. (Bristol, England, 1832), p. 18; William Chambers, *The Emigrant's Manual* (Edinburgh, 1851), p. 105; Theodore C. Blegan, ed., *The Land of Their Choice: The Immigrants Write Home* (Minneapolis, 1955), pp. 233–234.

[29]E. L. Jordan, tr. and ed., *America, Glorious and Chaotic Land:*

"The only place in Ireland where a man can make a fortune is America."[30]

Such exaggerations might be questioned, but who could doubt the testimony of former neighbors when their America letters recited their success stories in simple prose: "We sold our farm last winter for $800"; "We have five horses, seventeen cattle, thirteen sheep, and twenty-four hogs"; "I have deposited $800 in the bank"; "Our farm is worth five or six thousand dollars"; "I have 140 acres of land fenced, and nearly 30 under a good state of improvement."[31] A Japanese guidebook promised, "After five or six years, the person having no pennies will become a very rich man."[32]

The universality of this image of frontier prosperity was attested by ballad makers, who carried the promises of the image makers into the realm of absurdity. In the West of their creation lay a new Eden where "the hedges consist of sides of bacon and tobacco, so that you may lie in the shade of the bacon and smoke the tobacco"; where "tea and coffee and clotted cream fairly drown the settlers, pork and wheat are one's daily bread, and everyone lolls on the lap of fortune."[33] Throughout Scandinavia peasants sang—and still sing—the interminable verses of "Oleana":

Charles Sealsfield Discovers Young United States (Englewood Cliffs, N.J., 1969), p. 45.

30Quoted in Arnold Schrier, Ireland and the American Emigration, 1850–1900 (Minneapolis, 1958), p. 20.

31George M. Stephenson, ed., "Typical American Letters," Yearbook of the Swedish Historical Society of America 7 (1921–1922): 72, 73, 77, 8–, 82.

32Quoted in Watanabe, "Japanese Images," p. 4.

33Blegan, Land of Their Choice, p. 303; Blegan, Norwegian Emigrant Songs, p. 69.

They give you land for nothing in jolly Oleana
And grain comes leaping from the ground in
    floods of golden manna.
The grain it does the threshing, it pours into
    the sack, Sir,
So you can take a quiet nap, a-stretching on
    your back, Sir.
The little roasted piggies, with manners quite
    demure, Sir,
They ask, "Will you have some ham?" and
    then you say, "Why sure, Sir."[34]

To reach that land of promise was the "collective utopian dream" of thousands.[35]

Yet even more important to the image of the West than the lure of abundance was the promise of equality and freedom. If any phrase appeared more often in America letters than "We eat meat three times a day," it was, "Here we tip our hats to no one." In a new land where men were few and necessary tasks many, all who worked were respected, no matter how menial their duties. The manual laborer contributed to society no less than the merchant or lawyer and deserved to be treated in the same way. "Here," wrote a recent immigrant, "workingmen are not afraid of their masters; they are seen as equals."[36]

Such class distinctions as did exist, all agreed, were

34Blegan, ed., *Land of Their Choice*, pp. 282–283.

35René Dubos, "The Despairing Optimist," *American Scholar* 43 (Autumn, 1974): 545.

36Quoted in Charlotte Erickson, "Agrarian Myths of English Immigrants," in *In the Trek of the Immigrants*, ed. Oscar F. Ander (Rock Island, Ill., 1964), pp. 70–71.

based on wealth instead of lineage. What a man was, not what his family had been, determined his place in society. "Out West," a British visitor reported, "the one question asked is 'What can you do?' not 'Who was your father?' " Another, who mentioned ancestors to a frontiersman, was told, "We don't vally those things in this country; it's what's above ground, not what's under, that we think on."[37] Given these standards, a place in the upper crust of society awaited all who were enterprising. Gentlemen could be made of the coarsest stuff in a land where a fortunate speculation could overnight transform the village pauper into the community's richest, and hence most respected, citizen. "In Europe," Germans were told, "a man works to live; here he works to become rich."[38]

With equality went liberty—the liberty to think and act as one chose. "Here," a recent arrival wrote his old neighbors, "no emperor and no king has the right to command us to do anything."[39] Where all were equal, all governed; a common citizen had the right to slander and damn his government, abuse public officials to their faces, and call the president of the United States a fool without calling down the wrath of his fellows or the firm hand of the law. "Here I am free," was a repeated phrase in America letters.[40]

[37]Joseph Hatton, *To-day in America* (London, 1881), II, 38–39; Alexander Mackay, *The Western World* (Philadelphia, 1849), II, 29.

[38]Joseph A. von Hübner, *Promenade autour du Monde, 1871* (Paris, 1871), quoted in *This Was America*, ed. Oscar O. Handlin (Cambridge, Mass., 1949), p. 323.

[39]Berthold Auerbach, quoted in Weber, *America in Imaginative German Literature*, p. 200.

[40]Frederick L. Olmsted, *A Journey through Texas; or, A Saddletrip on the Southwestern Frontier* (New York, 1857), p. 282. Olmsted quotes a German settler who made this remark.

Personal independence was so venerated that it was sometimes asserted in extreme form. A traveler who objected to the off-key singing of a boatman was told that "he was in a land of liberty" and had no right to interfere.[41] A lad on the Illinois frontier, scolded by his mother for appropriating a piece of cake, answered: "Why, Mother, aren't we in a free country now?"[42] Another young man, ordered by his father to fetch some wood, was heard to say, "Go get it yourself, you old son of a bitch." The father turned to the witness, his face aglow with satisfaction. "A sturdy republican, sir," he said.[43] Absurdities, perhaps, but they mirrored the outlawing of subserviency on the frontier.

Such were the mores of republicanism reported by image makers that any social distinctions were vigorously opposed by frontiersmen. This seemed logical; in a land where abundance was within the reach of the most humble, there could be no humble. Travelers soon learned that they risked insult, if not injury, if they forgot that simple fact. One titled Englishman, hunting in Colorado, asked his guide to fill the tub in which he bathed. The guide suggested that he take a swim in the Platte River, then exploded, "You ain't quite the top-shelfer you think you is. You ain't even got a shower-bath for cooling your swelled head. But I'll make you a present of one, boss!" With that he pulled his revolver

41James Flint, *Letters from America* (Edinburgh, Scotland, 1822), p. 85.

42Quoted in George M. Stephenson, "When America Was the Land of Canaan," *Minnesota History* 10 (September, 1929): 254–255.

43William French, *Some Recollections of a Western Ranchman, New Mexico, 1883–1889* (London, 1927), p. 69; Richard L. Rapson, *Britons View America: Travel Commentary, 1860–1935* (Seattle, 1971), p. 99.

and shot the tub full of holes.[44] Often told were tales of the traveler who sent for a tailor to be measured for a coat and was told that such a procedure was not republican; of the serving maid who refused to allow her mistress to ring for her unless she could ring for the mistress whenever "she desired to have speech with her"; of the hostler who, when requested to call a guest in the morning, shouted, "Call yourself and be damned."[45]

Titles were taboo in that egalitarian society. All men were "Mister" and referred to each other as "gentlemen"; all women were "Madam" or "Miss" and were universally called "ladies."[46] Travelers from less democratic lands never tired of listing examples of frontier usage: the coachman who asked his passenger, "Are you the man going to Portland because if you are, I'm the gentleman that's going to drive you"; the frontier landlord who asked a group of stagecoach drivers, "Which is the gentleman who brought this man here?"; the court defendant who testified that "he and another gentleman had been shoveling mud"; the newspaper report of "two gentlemen who were convicted and sentenced to six months' imprisonment for horse stealing."[47]

Personal relationships were as democratized as

[44]William A. Baillie-Groham, *Fifteen Years' Sport and Life in the Hunting Grounds of Western America and British Columbia* (London, 1900), pp. 4–5.

[45]Marryat, *Diary in America*, II, 155; T. C. Grattan, *Civilized America* (London, 1859), I, 268; Adlard Welby, *A Visit to North America and the English Settlements in Illinois* (London, 1821), p. 35.

[46]Hübner, *Promenade autour du Monde*, quoted in Handlin, ed., *This Was America*, p. 301; Flint, *Letters from America*, pp. 169–170.

[47]Tyrone Power, *Impressions of America During the Years 1833, 1834, and 1835* (London, 1836), I, 286; Charles Lyell, *Travels in North America* (London, 1845), I, 49; Simon A. Ferrell, *A Ramble of Six Thousand Miles Through the United States of America* (London, 1832), p. 308.

forms of address, according to the image makers, particularly in frontier inns, where laborers and judges, drovers and merchants, magistrates and stagecoach drivers dined side by side, waited on by "helps" (the word *servant* was never used) who addressed them by their first names, leaned over their chairs to take part in the conversation, and shed their coats to join in a game of cards when the meal was over.[48] This social freedom was offensive enough to class-conscious visitors, but worse was the application of democratic principles to sleeping arrangements. Guests were assigned to beds in the order of their arrival, with two, three, or four in each bed. Judges snored next to teamsters, legislators beside wagoners, and bankers with hog drivers as their partners. "A most almighty beautiful democratic amalgam," one westerner was heard to call the system.[49] But it was hardly pleasing to the fastidious, for guests were changed more often than the sheets. One who objected was rudely reminded, "Since *Gentlemen* are all alike, people do not see why they should not sleep in the same sheets."[50]

The image makers who pictured the American frontier for their readers performed their task well. By the 1890's, wrote a Czech publicist, "the most illiterate peasant in the Balkans, who did not even know the name of his county-seat, knew about America, about its free land and the absence of landlords."[51] That peasant knew, as did others throughout much of the world, that

48Katona, "Hungarian Travelogues," pp. 75–76.
49William Kelly, *A Stroll Through the Diggings* (London, 1852), p. 47.
50Ferdinand M. Bayard, *Travels of a Frenchman in Maryland and Virginia* (Ann Arbor, Mich., 1950), p. 36.
51Quoted in Peter Drucker, *The End of Economic Man* (New York, 1939), pp. 42–43.

the American West was a land of abundance and opportunity, of equality and freedom, where land was assured to the industrious and where the upper ranks of society were open to the humble. "A nation of sovereigns," an Irish newspaper called it with some reason.[52]

The projection of this image played a role, no matter how minor, in stirring the spirit of rebellion that underlay many of the economic, social, and political reforms of the late nineteenth and early twentieth centuries. Peasant farmers in Europe who learned of a land where all ate meat three times daily and tipped their hats to no one would no longer accept their subservient role with the same docile humility. Their horizons had been widened and their ambitions stirred by visions of a better life. "This people," wrote a Swedish publicist, "which has for so many years been satisfied with its meagre lot, has begun to reason with itself, and has found that things could be better than they are."[53] The seeds of discontent had been planted, and only domestic reforms could keep them in check.

Those reforms remade many of the Old World's institutions, but nowhere did the frontier image play a more important role than in the debate over the right of men—all men—to govern themselves. Liberals and conservatives agreed that the poor in the American West were better off than those in the Old World. They disagreed on the reasons why. Liberals, favoring reform,

[52]*Limerick Reporter*, August 29, 1873, quoted in Schrier, *Ireland and the American Emigration*, p. 19.

[53]Quoted in Franklin D. Scott, "Sweden's Constructive Opposition to Emigration," *Journal of Modern History* 37 (September, 1965): 310.

insisted that the higher living standards in the West were the product of democratic institutions; the frontier was a paradise for small-farmers because small-farmers shaped its policies. Liberalize government in the Old World, they said, and it will reward the liberalizers with the same affluence enjoyed by the New.[54]

Conservatives answered that American prosperity and equality were the products solely of cheap western lands and hence were beyond the grasp of settled nations. Manhood suffrage succeeded simply because the frontier drained workers from the East, thus intensifying competition for jobs and elevating the wages of those who remained while at the same time siphoning off the discontented, who posed the greatest threat to the social system. Cheap lands also equalized the ownership of property, allowing the majority a stake in society, and with landownership went the sense of social responsibility necessary for a stable electorate. Older nations, with no reservoir of occupiable land, were unsuited to democracy. Wrote the editor of England's *Quarterly Review*: "The inexhaustible fund of unoccupied land . . . exempts the great body of the lower classes from what in other countries is the most usual and fruitful source of popular discontent and tumult, namely, the pressure of want."[55]

The effectiveness of this argument was demonstrat-

[54]The controversy over the English reform bills of 1832 and 1867 is explored in terms of this concept in G. D. Lillibridge, *Beacon of Freedom: The Impact of American Democracy upon Great Britain, 1830–1870* (Philadelphia, 1955), and William M. Tuttle, Jr., "Forerunners of Frederick Jackson Turner: Nineteenth-Century British Conservatives and the Frontier Thesis," *Agricultural History* 41 (July, 1967): 219–227.

[55]*Quarterly Review* 46 (January, 1832): 584–585.

ed by reformers in Denmark, Sweden, Norway, and Prussia when they acknowledged the validity of the frontier as a safety valve by trying to create artificial frontiers to drain away excess workers and raise the living standard of the remainder. In Denmark this ambition helps explain the *Husmand* movement, which was designed to parcel great estates among small holders; in Norway and Sweden it underlay an effort to drain swamplands and open hitherto unoccupied northern territories to peasants; in Prussia it was directed toward dividing the giant Junker holdings. These moves failed, but their popularity suggests that the image of the American frontier as a land of promise was not lost on social critics in older countries.[56]

No one would suggest that the frontier image was solely or even largely responsible for the social, economic, and political changes that altered Old World institutions during the dawning years of the present century. Yet there seems to be little question that that image bred discontent among the least advantaged classes in Europe (and to a lesser degree in Asia) and helped set in motion the alterations that eventually bettered their lot. The image makers, whether exuberant

[56]This subject deserves more extensive investigation. The importance of the findings awaiting researchers is suggested in Halvdan Koht, *The American Spirit in Europe* (Philadelphia, 1949); Ingrid Semmingsen, "Emigration and the Image of Europe," in *Immigration and American History: Essays in Honor of Theodore C. Blegan*, ed. Henry S. Commager (Minneapolis, 1961); Folke Dovring, "European Reactions to the Homestead Act," *Journal of Economic History* 22 (December, 1962): 461–472; Brynjolf J. Hovde, "Notes on the Effects of Emigration upon Scandinavia," *Journal of Modern History* 6 (September, 1934): 253–279; and especially the stimulating studies of Franklin D. Scott, *Emigration and Immigration*, 2d ed. (Washington, D.C., 1966), and "American Influences in Norway and Sweden," *Journal of Modern History* 18 (March, 1946): 37–47.

guidebook writers, land promoters, imaginative novelists, travelers, or the homespun authors of America letters, helped shape the course of history, and they deserve a larger place in its annals than they have been accorded.